CAMARO
AN AMERICAN ICON

BY GARY WITZENBURG

AND THE AUTO EDITORS OF CONSUMER GUIDE®

Publications International, Ltd.

Credits

Photography:

The editors would like to thank the following people and organizations for supplying the photography that made this book possible. They are listed below, along with the page number(s) of their photos.

Jeff Cohn: 38, 39, 52; **Steve Fecht:** 144; **Fineprint Productions:** 148, 150, 159; **Mitch Frumkin:** 105; **Sam Griffith:** 17, 34, 40, 41, 118, 119; **Martin Gross:** 25; **Brandon Hemphill:** 35; **Jimmy Huston:** 55; **IMS Photo:** 21, 116, 123; **Bud Juneau:** 26; **Nick Komic:** 22, 30, 31, 42, 43; **Dan Lyons:** 19; **Vince Manocchi:** 18, 19, 90, 93, 126; **John F. Martin:** 147, 154; **Doug Mitchel:** 28, 57, 61, 64, 68, 70, 72, 133; **Mike Mueller:** 20; **Robert Nicholson:** 85; **David Noles:** 151; **Tom Pidgeon:** 143, 146; **Jeffrey Sauger:** 144; **David Temple:** 54, 71, 100, 105; **Phil Toy:** 36, 37; **Nicky Wright:** 99

Contents: Jeff Cohn
Foreword: Phil Toy
Chapter Opener Illustrations by Frank Peiler: 9, 45, 77, 107, 135

Owners:

Special thanks to the owners of the cars featured in this book for their cooperation. Their names and the page number(s) for their vehicles follow.

Jackie Bean: 100; **Tom Bigelow:** 19; **Jerry and Carol Buczkowski:** 99; **Mitch Deck:** 70; **John DeLoach:** 105; **Duffy's Collectible Cars:** 85; **Rob Embleton:** 17, 34, 40, 41; **Mark Knecht:** Contents; 38, 39; **Paul McGuire:** 20; **Randy Mitchell:** 52; **Ann Mocklin:** 72; **Bob Lichty/Motorcar Portfolio, LLC:** 35; **Jason Newman:** 100; **John R. Oehler:** 28, 57, 61, 64, 68; **Tom Pellett:** 54; **Ramshead Auto Collection:** 26; **Ron and Laureen Roach:** Foreword; 36, 37; **Steve Schultz/SS Classic Cars:** 22, 30, 31, 42, 43; **Ralph Segars:** 71; **Howard and Yvonne Van Der Eb:** 18, 19

Our appreciation to the historical archives and media services groups at General Motors Corporation and the Gilmore Car Museum.

About The Auto Editors of Consumer Guide®:

For more than 40 years, Consumer Guide® has published new-car buying guides, including the trusted bimonthly *Car & Truck Test*.

The Consumer Guide® staff drives and evaluates more than 200 vehicles annually.

Consumerguide.com is one of the web's most popular automotive resources, visited by 2.5 million shoppers monthly.

The Auto Editors of Consumer Guide® also publish the award-winning bimonthly *Collectible Automobile®* magazine.

CONTENTS

FOREWORD

The Chevrolet Camaro has been an American icon since it first hit the street for 1967. Though a belated response to the hugely successful Ford Mustang, the Chevy "ponycar" attracted a large, devoted following all its own. The racing-inspired Z28 and its winning track exploits only added to the mystique. Moreover, Camaro remained true to its mission even as daunting new realities in the 1970s caused other ponycars to disappear or become far less compelling.

Consistency has played a big part in Camaro's long-running popularity. For example, the "1970½" second-generation design lasted a dozen years, thanks to adept and timely updates that not only kept it fresh, but right in step with changing public attitudes and government regulations. The redesigned 1982 third generation led a renaissance for Detroit performance with new technology in a leaner, meaner package. A decade of steady gains in power and panache set the stage for a fourth generation combining even higher performance with dramatic showcar styling and new levels of refinement and sophistication.

Yet through all these memorable years of RS, SS, Z28, and IROC-Z models, Camaro production never topped that of the archrival Mustang. Worse, demand tailed off as Americans began flocking to sport-utility vehicles, prompting GM to abandon ponycars after 2002. But Camaro was too good to lose, and within a few years it would be reborn as a 21st-century sports car that honors its past while looking confidently to the future.

Camaro: An American Icon chronicles a living-legend automobile that's respected and desired the world over. It's a great story. Enjoy!

1

Ford's Mustang set the automotive world afire when it galloped on the American scene in April 1964. In fact, it forced Chevy to respond for 1967 with the Camaro, but the truth is that Chevrolet had been toying with the "ponycar" concept since 1962.

FIRST GENERATION: CHALLENGES AND CHOICES

Most of us know the first Camaro as Chevrolet's hurry-up answer to Ford's astoundingly popular Falcon-based Mustang, which had been launched to thunderous applause and sell-out status in April 1964. And while GM missed the message at first, it soon stepped up to the challenge and approved design and development of what became the 1967 Camaro.

Super Nova

But did you know that Chevy designers had been toying with essentially the same idea since soon after the debut of the first compact Chevy II for 1962? Then-Chevrolet Chief Designer Irv Rybicki, while observing the creation of Buick's first '63 Riviera "personal coupe," got the bright idea that a smaller, more affordable sporty coupe built on the Chevy II platform might be a good idea for Chevrolet. He proposed it to GM Styling Vice President Bill Mitchell, and Mitchell agreed.

Wanting to keep the project under wraps, they set up a secret studio in a warehouse across the street and put some designers and sculptors to work. Five months later, they had a clay model close to the (still-unknown) Mustang in size and proportion. So close that Rybicki later said, "it was astounding . . . and we didn't even know those devils at Ford were doing one."

Mitchell was impressed, so he showed it to then-Chevrolet General Manager S. E. "Bunkie" Knudsen. Knudsen liked it but decided not to pursue it. With the upcoming introduction of the mid-size Chevelle for 1964, he reasoned, Chevy would have five separate car lines. It surely did not need a sixth.

But Rybicki didn't give up on the idea. Late in 1963, he had Hank Haga's Chevrolet #2 Studio design a Chevy II-based concept car called Super Nova. It was a handsome, low-profile, sporty coupe with a long hood,

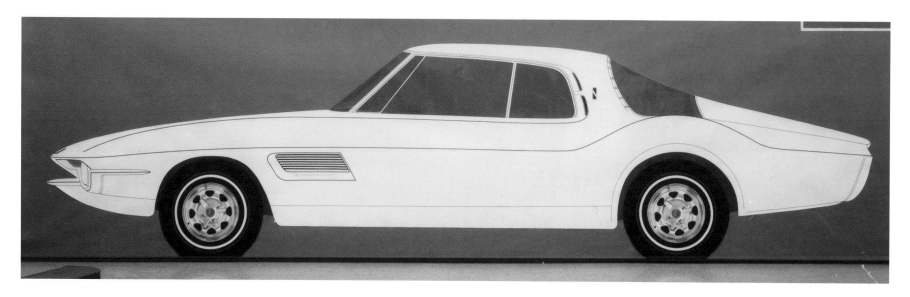

short deck, and minimal chrome. Mitchell liked it so much he had it developed into a fiberglass-bodied running car and dispatched it to the 1964 New York Auto Show for a public unveiling . . . several weeks before the Mustang's storied debut.

And it created a stir, especially from Ford folks. "It was an idea car," Knudsen said, "but not so exotic that you couldn't produce it. I recall some Ford people coming over while I was standing there and asking whether we were going to build it. And I remarked, 'If they'll let us, we'll build it.' I think that shook them up a bit, because it was a pretty good-looking little car."

Rybicki downplayed the Super Nova as, "just a concept piece, to see what reaction we'd get from the public . . . and the reaction was fairly good. I remember Knudsen came back talking about it and wondering how he could sell it [to GM upper management]." But then-President Jack Gordon turned it down. "That left us with nothing but the Corvair," Knudsen lamented.

The Corvair was due for a very nice redesign for 1965, so corporate

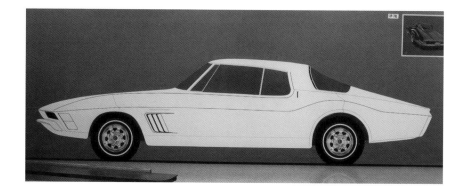

Early styling studies, from May and October 1962. Though they exhibit the appropriate long hood/short deck proportions, these drawings seem more suggestive of luxury tourers than what later became known as ponycars. Though the overall dimensions stay about the same, note the many variations in fender shapes, rooflines, vent styling, and other details between the drawings. Designers used blown-up photos of real wheels to lend detail and realism to their quickly-rendered sketches.

Opposite: The Chevy II-based Super Nova concept car was unveiled at the 1964 New York Auto Show. Public reaction was mostly favorable, but GM upper management nixed production plans. The Corvair-based Monza SS concept roadster is seen in the background of the color photo. *This page:* A selection of styling studies from 1964 shows the Camaro's design progression. At the top, a clay model exhibiting a fast-back-like roofline is compared to a Ford Mustang fastback and Chevy's own Corvair Monza. In the bottom photos, the fastback shape has evolved into a more formal roofline. The clay model at the right exhibits a more upright nose and tail—a bit closer to the production car.

leaders believed its sporty new look and optional turbocharged engine would help it compete quite well against this new sporty car from Ford. But while GM brass kept its collective head in the sand throughout most of that first summer of Mustang mania, it became increasingly obvious that something would have to be done. Mitchell was saying publicly that the '65 Corvair was Chevy's answer to the Mustang, but Rybicki had Haga's studio working on new sporty concepts, and Knudsen kept trying to sell the idea at monthly Engineering Policy Committee meetings.

It took just four months for Ford's Mustang to top 100,000 sales on its

way to the biggest first-year success of any new car in history. And it took those first 100,000 sold-out Mustangs to awaken GM's conservative corporate management.

Sleeping Giant

But a sleeping giant, once aroused, can move pretty fast. When the corporate light finally turned green that August, it was less than two years before Chevy's Mustang rival would have to be in production for a fall 1966 introduction. The mandate was clear: It would have to out-gun Mustang in every dimension: longer, lower, wider, roomier, faster, smoother, better-handling. Yet it would have to be based on the upcoming '68 redesigned compact Chevy II/Nova platform, using as many off-the-shelf parts as possible to keep costs down.

Haga's studio, which had been working on sporty four-seat concepts all along, got the assignment to create the production design. "The people in the studio—designers modelers and engineers alike—were all enthusiasts," Haga said. "They were pretty excited when they found they had a chance to design an all-new four-place sports car, which would eventually compete directly with the Ford Mustang. We had a lot of artwork on the wall.

Top and far left: An interior mockup from late 1964 shows a bit of Corvette influence. Console-mounted control knobs are an unusual idea that never saw production. *Left:* Hidden headlamps identified Camaros equipped with the Rally Sport appearance package. As this photo shows, grille sections at each end powered aside to uncover the lamps.

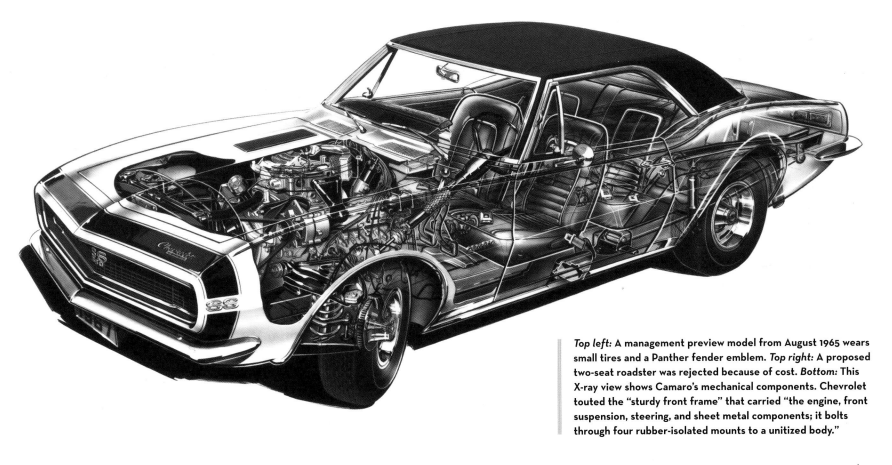

Top left: A management preview model from August 1965 wears small tires and a Panther fender emblem. *Top right:* A proposed two-seat roadster was rejected because of cost. *Bottom:* This X-ray view shows Camaro's mechanical components. Chevrolet touted the "sturdy front frame" that carried "the engine, front suspension, steering, and sheet metal components; it bolts through four rubber-isolated mounts to a unitized body."

After a speedy design and engineering process, Camaro was launched on-schedule on September 12, 1966. The enormous options list was daunting, but enabled Camaro shoppers to create a mild-mannered cruiser, a swingin' performance machine, or anything in between. *Opposite page:* A 1967 Camaro convertible priced from $2704 with a 140-hp 230-cid six, $2809 with base 210-hp 327 V-8. The Bolero Red example shown here is equipped with the optional 155-hp "Turbo-Thrift" 250-cid six, which added $26.35 to the bottom line.

We knew it was going to happen someday because those Mustangs were out there creating a lot of excitement in the marketplace. It was hot and heavy in our studio once we got the word. We were really flying, did a lot of renderings and put in a lot of overtime."

Exterior

Starting with designs similar to what had evolved from Rybicki's short-lived "warehouse" project sporty coupe two years before, Haga and Assistant Studio Chief John Schinella soon had their own ideas molded in clay for three-dimensional viewing. The theme was "fluid," looking like canvas stretched over wire, the dominant GM design direction at that time.

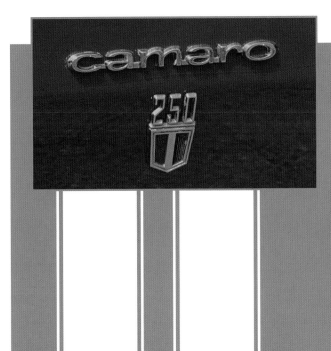

THE NAME

As late as the spring of 1966, just a few months before Chevy's long-awaited Mustang rival was due to debut, it still did not have a name.

"We were in the process of tooling, and we nearly completed the car with four different names," relates then-Chevrolet Engineering Director Alex Maier. "We had a whole bunch of names, and it was almost the start of production when we decided to name it Camaro. With the Ford name being Mustang, I think we had at least a couple of animal names. Panther was one of them. I think we tooled that. Wildcat was another."

But auto safety advocates were attacking aggressive animal names at the time, "and there was pressure at Chevrolet to use something starting with 'C,' Maier continued. "Corvette, Corvair, Chevy II, Chevelle—almost all of our names did at the time, and that policy had been very successful. Also, even though it was a sporty car, Chevrolet thought that names should have a good, soft, even feminine sound, not harsh."

Chevy employees suggested some 5000 names, none of which seemed suitable, before Assistant General Sales Manager Bob Lund and GM Car and Truck Group Vice President Ed Rollert came up with Camaro. "I wanted to name it Chaparral," says Lund [after the famous Chevy-powered Chaparral race cars], "but I wasn't able to do so. I submitted a lot of names and couldn't get any approved. Finally it got to the point where we were desperate. We had to have a name to make the tools.

"One morning, Ed Rollert and I got together and went over all the names that had been submitted for consideration. We had English-French and English-Spanish dictionaries and a copy of *Roget's Thesaurus*. Finally, I found this word "Camaro," which had kind of a ring, a dramatic sound to it, and I said, 'Here's a hell of a name!' I read him the various definitions of it, one of which was very appropriate — friend, warm friend, something of that nature."

Thus Camaro it would be.

—*Gary Witzenburg*

How did they come up with the bumblebee striping around the SS model's nose? "We started looking at some fighter planes," Haga explained, "and they had a black, non-reflective panel on top of the nose so the pilot wouldn't get reflections off the bare aluminum. Some also had a sort of bumblebee stripe around the air intake. So we applied that to our nose. One reason was that it tended to visually shorten the nose and made it look a little tougher."

"We did a million different taillights," Schinella joked, trying for the right rear appearance. The traditional Chevrolet round lamps "didn't locate right," Haga said. "It still looked too much like a sedan, and round taillights looked a little out of place. We wanted to get a bigger lens area on that car. Also we were trying to stay away from the Corvair look."

Early in 1965, the taut Coke-bottle body shape was wind-tunnel tested

Opposite and above left: SS Camaros got stiffer springs and shocks, F70 × 14 Firestone Wide Oval tires, performance hood with dual dummy exhaust vents, and "bumblebee" nose stripes. A 295-hp 350 was available from the start, and a 375-hp 396 was added in November 1966. *Left:* In addition to the hidden-headlamp grille, the $105.35 Rally Sport option package included RS badges, full taillamps with separate under-bumper backup lights, bright rocker/drip rail/wheel arch moldings, and black rocker bottoms.

for drag, lift, side forces, pitch, roll, and yaw, and minor changes resulted. The front fenders and lower valence shapes, for example, were altered slightly to improve aerodynamic flow and directional stability and reduce drag from turbulence.

The basic car featured what Chevy described as a "jet engine" nose opening with a fine eggcrate-pattern grille and round parking lamps inboard of larger round headlamps. The optional RS (Rally Sport) front had pivoting headlamp covers blending into a larger-mesh black-out grille and rectangular parking lamps in the valence below the bumper. Specific side trim, taillamp treatments, and RS identification were included in the package.

Opposite: Bowing in early 1967, the Camaro Z-28 package was created for the Sports Car Club of America's year-old Trans-American race series for compact "sedans." Included were broad dorsal stripes, "Rally" wheels, wide red-stripe tires, and uprated F41 suspension. The heart of the package was a special high-tune, high-winding 302 V-8, basically the 327 block running a 283 V-8 crankshaft. Left: In another ploy to publicize its new Mustang fighter, Chevrolet lobbied officials at the Indianapolis Motor Speedway to choose Camaro as pace car for the 1967 Indy 500. The actual pacer was this RS/SS 396 convertible, but about 100 replicas were built with 350 V-8s and Powerglide transmissions for official use during race week. All were later sold to the public.

THE TIRES

There was considerable controversy over the '67 Camaro's base tires and wheels. Standard Chevrolet procedure at the time was to start with small, inexpensive, barely adequate rubber and work up from there to more substantial optional tire and wheel combinations. But the Camaro's designers and engineers both wanted a higher level of standard equipment.

"When you start any kind of passenger car program," Chief Designer Hank Haga said, "you put together the tire and wheel sizes that the final car will run on, and this car was treated just like any sedan. It had to have that wide variety of tire sizes like any ordinary car. But when you put the smallest tire into the wheel openings necessary for the biggest tire, it looked horrible.

"One day we had our fiberglass model together and reviewed it out at the Proving Grounds, and it looked like a car on roller skates. It looked so bad, we were just sick about it, and the implication was that we had designed it that way. Well, we had designed it the best we could with the objectives we had. If we could have dropped that little tire and had a larger standard tire and wheel, it would've worked out much better."

As a young Chevrolet engineer when the '67 Camaro hit the streets, I remember feeling great about it and believing it was indeed better than its hot-selling Ford rival in nearly every way. But I also remember thinking how silly the base car looked on its skinny little tires, and wondering what our leaders were thinking when they specified them. Of course, it was standard operating procedure, as Haga said, and it helped achieve the very low base price.

Fortunately, few dealers or buyers ordered it that way.

—Gary Witzenburg

Interior

Meanwhile, Assistant Chief Designer George Angersbach's Chevy #2 Interior Studio was struggling with an instrument panel that had to look better and sportier than the Chevy II's but could not cost much more to produce. He mounted a four-speed shift handle on the side of his chair to remind himself that he was working on a performance-oriented car and developed a very attractive concept similar to that in the Super Nova show car. It featured three separate round pods housing a speedometer and tachometer on either side of a large clock, with smaller auxiliary gauges high in a large center console extension that swept up from the floor.

This concept was later toned down to a less-expensive design with two large portholes for speedometer and tach and three small, optional gauges mounted low on a shorter, plainer console. "It had some of the flavor of the Corvair," Angersbach said, "and also some from Corvette. We

Opposite: As the muscle-car craze reached its zenith, many new-car dealerships doubled as speed shops, and a few even produced their own special-edition cars. Yenko Chevrolet in Canonsburg, Pennsylvania, fitted a small run of 1967 Camaros with 425-hp Corvette 427 V-8s. This Butternut Yellow example wears a fiberglass hood, '67 Corvette side exhaust pipes, and the Rally Sport package. *This page:* Chevrolet wasted no time conjuring concept Camaros for the auto show circuit. Pictured here are the Waikiki, replete with "woody" side panels, Cibie square headlights, and Dayton wire wheels; the Cherokee, which packed a Weber-carbed 396 under its clear-bubble hood scoop; and the Caribe, a novel "roadster pickup" with a targa bar separating the cockpit and bed.

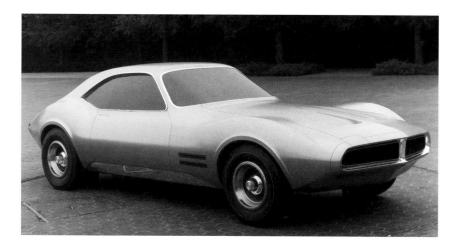

were doing a new Corvette instrument panel at the time, which didn't fly, so we used part of that design on the Camaro. At first, the gauges were on the instrument panel and located high, but they slipped down onto the console when they became optional."

Engineering Development

The Camaro's development engineers were faced with the challenge of creating a car based upon, yet very different from, the Chevy II. "We had a rather aggressive development group at the time," relates then-development engineer Paul King. "We had a lot of facilities and did a lot of investigating of different kinds of structural concepts, arrangement concepts, and suspension concepts." Fortunately, because the Chevy II would be superseded by an all-new model for 1968, they were working with a much-better body/chassis platform.

This new architecture eventually evolved into a clever combination of the two basic types of automobile construction: body-frame integral ("unibody") and separate frame. A partial frame, looking like the front portion of a conventional ladder frame, became the platform on which the entire front structure—inner and outer sheet metal, engine, transmission, suspen-

Top: Camaro's first generation had not yet bowed when GM stylists were already at work on refinements and changes. The clays seen here date from August 1966. *Bottom:* A crisper, more formal roofline and an integral "ducktail" spoiler are evident in this September 1966 sketch. *Opposite left:* This racy mock-up from July '66 wears Halibrand wheels, flat black hood paint, SS stripes, and "Chaparral" badging. *Opposite right:* This pre-production Rally Sport coupe has dummy front fender vents that never made production.

TRANS AM RACING SUCCESS

The year 1967 saw the U.S. ponycar wars explode with debuts of GM's Chevy Camaro, Pontiac's Firebird, a new Plymouth Barracuda and a Mustang-based Mercury Cougar. And with all but Plymouth jumping in with factory-supported teams and big-name drivers, the SCCA's Trans Am racing series grew to a dozen hard-fought events.

Jerry Titus' Mustang won four to bring Ford its second championship ahead of corporate cousin Mercury, while Mark Donohue won three in Roger Penske's Camaro. Among the other notable drivers were Peter Revson, Dan Gurney, David Pearson, Parnelli Jones, George Follmer, Ed Leslie, Cale Yarborough, Lee Roy Yarbrough, Milt Minter, Bob Grossman, Ronnie Bucknum, Bob Bondurant, and Jerry Grant.

The annual Daytona 24-Hour was the 1968 season-opening event, and Titus and Bucknum co-drove to a win for Mustang. But then the Penske/Donohue machine kicked into gear and spun off eight straight victories to clinch the championship for Chevrolet. Titus took one and Horst Kwech another for Ford, then Donohue won two more to rub it in.

Thanks to the intense factory competition and the famous drivers it attracted, this new series was great fun to watch—sideways-drifting, fender-banging, tire-smoking terrific racing of the highest order. "A Trans Am race is hard to drive from the standpoint of physical input," Donohue told a reporter at the time. "The cars are very strong, you can push them further than you can more fragile racing machinery, so it becomes a very grueling kind of race."

Embarrassed by Chevy's dominance in 1968, Ford fielded two factory teams for '69: a Shelby Mustang for Revson and twin Bud Moore entries for Jones and Follmer. Parnelli won the opener, and Sam Posey the next one in a Shelby Mustang. Bucknum's Camaro took the third race, then Jones and Follmer bagged one each to make it four out of five for Ford. But Donohue's Camaro won six of the last seven, and the one he didn't, Bucknum's Camaro did.

That locked the second-straight title for Chevrolet.

—*Gary Witzenburg*

This page and opposite bottom: A revised grille with rectangular parking lamps freshened the appearance of all '68 Camaros without the hidden headlamp RS package. *Opposite top:* This view of the '68 Camaro dash shows the outboard air registers that were part of the new flow-through "Astro Ventilation" system, which dispensed with the door vent windows on all of that year's models.

sion, brakes, steering—was assembled. This unit extended under the rear unibody under the front seat area and was bolted to it through tuned rubber mounts.

The front suspension used short upper and long, wide, wishbone-type lower control arms with tube shocks inside coil springs mounted between the lower arms and a structural suspension crossmember. Steering was a parallel relay recirculating-ball design mounted aft of the suspension. Standard brakes were 9.5-inch drums with 2.5-inch-wide front linings and 2.0-inch-wide in the rear. The Hotchkiss rear layout suspended its solid rear axle on single leaf "mono-plate" springs that were shorter than the Chevy II's and splayed outward front to rear to make room for the 18-gallon

gas tank. Its rear tube shocks were outboard of the springs, near-vertical in base-suspension cars and staggered in the SS 350 performance version.

Several new safety features, most of them required by law on 1967 models, were incorporated into the design. These included a mesh-type collapsible steering column, dual hydraulic braking circuits divided front and rear, a brake system warning light, four-way hazard flashers, front-seat backrest latches and built-in attachments for optional front seat shoulder harnesses. One innovative convenience feature was a new lane change signal activated by moving the turn signal lever to a position just short of the detent in either direction.

Opposite: Camaro's Z-28 package was more readily available for '68, but still far from common with just 7199 installations. In addition to the 302 V-8 with mandatory 4-speed manual, Z-28 improvements included quick-ratio steering, heavy-duty radiator, and dual deep-tone mufflers. *This page:* The Camaro's "bumble-bee" nose stripe continued, but was joined by a combination nose/bodyside stripe, as seen on this SS 350 convertible. The hood vents weren't functional, but the SS's 350 still managed to put out 295 horsepower with its 4-barrel carburetor and 10.25:1 compression ratio.

Yenko Chevrolet was still serving up its own special brand of "Super Camaro." As in 1967, proprietor Don Yenko would order SS 396 Camaros from the factory, then swap out the 375-hp L78 396 for a 425-hp L72 427. Heavy-duty suspension, a 4.10:1 Positraction rear end, and a 140-mph speedometer were specially installed at the factory. Yenko badges and a twin-scooped fiberglass hood with tie-down pins were also part of the package. It's estimated that just 65 of these boulevard beasties were built for '68. Most were equipped with Pontiac Rally II wheels with unique "Y" center caps.

The Build-up

On July 1, 1965, Knudsen was promoted into GM's corporate management and Pontiac General Manager Pete Estes moved over to Chevrolet to replace him. "The interior design was pretty well set by the time I got there," Estes recalled, "but we were still working on the front end and the rear end at that time.

"I remember when we took it off the Proving Grounds for test rides. We had the whole thing camouflaged, all blacked out with cardboard on the quarter panels and everything. But the fact that it was low and sleek and slender in the body prompted lots of questions. If a prototype car causes a big commotion, even looking like that, when you pull into a gas station or something, you really know you've got something. That was a hot car right from the start."

The car was first shown to sales, advertising and public relations (really media relations) executives that November, and most were highly enthusi-

astic. Though its early internal code name was XP-836, which later evolved to "F-car" in accordance with GM platform naming convention at the time, it had become universally known as "Panther" both inside and outside the company. (See the sidebar on page 17 for the saga of how it became "Camaro.")

At about that same time, the PR team began planning its July 1966 long-lead magazine preview, while the advertising and marketing groups started preliminary work on catalogs, direct mail and sales promotion materials along with ads for outdoor, print, and electronic media. The PR effort began in earnest early in 1966 with a program of close contact with high-circulation magazines to work out fall-issue features and cover illustrations. Prototypes and finished styling models were photographed extensively, and Chevrolet Engineering contributed detailed technical illustrations.

On June 29, 1966, Chevrolet took the unusual step of announcing the car's newly chosen name and revealing some basic information about it.

Opposite top: High-performance and racing seemed to be on everyone's mind in the mid-to-late Sixties. This swoopy rendering wears contingency sponsor stickers and the preferred number of legendary race-car engineering guru Smokey Yunick. *Opposite bottom:* Stylists were still playing with two-seater ideas in fall 1966. *This page:* Various 1967 design studies display styling elements that would appear on production 1969 Camaros as well as the 1970½ second-generation model. Note the sleek door handles; a similar (albeit thicker) design would show up on the production 1969 Pontiac Grand Prix.

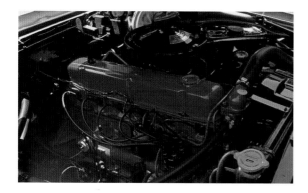

This page: Recontoured below-the-belt sheetmetal gave a huskier look to all 1969 Camaros. Again, two six-cylinder engines were offered: a 140-hp 230 (shown here) and a 155-hp 250. Both were handily outsold by the V-8s. The '69 Indy pace car was an eye-grabbing RS/SS Camaro ragtop with Hugger Orange stripes and an orange "houndstooth" interior. *Opposite:* "Hockey stick" stripes were a new dress-up option. Interior updates included a revised instrument panel with soft or recessed switchgear per federal safety mandates, along with a new stirrup-shaped shift lever.

One objective was to bury "Panther" once and for all. A huge conference call was arranged linking simultaneous press meetings in 14 different cities. Amplifiers and microphones allowed reporters to hear Estes' Detroit-based presentation, as well as each other, and to direct questions back to Detroit.

Calling it a "four-passenger package of excitement," Estes declared that "the Camaro is aimed at the fast-growing personal sports-type market that was pioneered by the Chevrolet Corvette in 1953 and further defined by the Corvair Monza in the 1960s." Because of its computer-aided design and development and its wind-tunnel-tested shape, he claimed that the new car was "perhaps more than any other automobile, a true product of the space age."

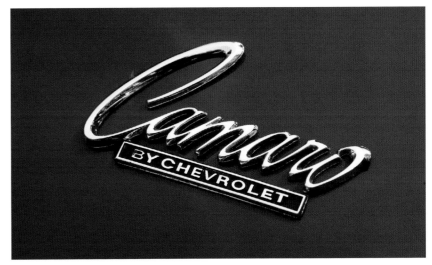

At one point, to add a colorful visual element to the program, a half-dozen Michigan State University cheerleaders bounced into the room, each carrying a huge letter card. While a narrator described the scene for those in the other cities, they arranged themselves to spell CAMARO. Unmentioned in the narrative was the fact that the last two lined up out of order at first, spelling "CAMAOR."

Estes told the press that Camaro meant "comrade," or "pal," in French, and "thus suggests the real mission of our new automobile . . . to be a close companion to its owner, tailored to reflect his or her individual tastes and at the same time provide exciting personal transportation."

The Rally Sport option package was carried over to the revamped-for-'69 Camaro body. It now included hidden headlamps with headlamp washers and triple glass windows for "flash-to-pass" signaling. The vacuum-operated headlamp covers powered aside for nighttime driving. Will the timeless good looks of a well-equipped 1969 Camaro ever go out of style? We don't think so.

Asked how he had come up with that name, he joked that he had locked himself in a closet just that morning and had come out with it. Later he quipped that a Camaro was a little-known animal "that lives on Mustangs."

On-time Launch

Following two years of flank-speed design and engineering work, the '67 Camaro coupe and convertible launched on schedule on September 12, 1966 . . . to mixed reviews. Critics praised their curvaceous, wind-tunnel-tuned styling, especially in hidden-headlamp Rally Sport (RS) and Super Sport (SS) trim, but panned the $2466 base car's skinny standard-equipment tires and wheels (see sidebar on page 21). Some called it a late-comer Mustang copy, and some mocked its soft, non-aggressive name.

Those first-year Camaros boasted several competitive advantages over '67 Mustangs, including the stiffer subframe front structure, wider tracks, more safety features, and higher quality paint. Both coupe and convertible could be ordered with the black-out grille, hidden-headlamp, special-trim RS option; and a 295-hp 350-cid small-block V-8-powered SS 350 package added heavy-duty suspension and the unique "bumblebee" nose striping.

Camaro's Z-28 package had fully come into its own by '69, and the sales figures proved it. Production nearly tripled, to 20,302. Mechanically, the package saw little change, but a bulged "cowl induction" hood was a new $79 option. It had a valve that snapped open at 80-percent throttle to draw in cool air from the base of the windshield. Factory-installed four-wheel disc brakes were optional on all Camaros this year, but only 206 got them; the $500 price tag likely discouraged shoppers.

But that year's Mustang offered three body styles (coupe, convertible, and fastback) to Camaro's two, and its 390 GT models were more powerful than Camaro's SS 350.

Magazine tests of the SS 350 reported 0-60 jaunts in the mid-7-second range, quarter-mile times around 16 seconds, and top speeds of 118-120 mph. Most liked its styling, ride, and handling, except for the rear axle's tendency to hop during pop-the-clutch drag-racing starts.

Before that first year was out, however, two exciting new engines were in: a high-revving 302 V-8 under-rated at 290 hp in the limited-production, road race-tuned Z-28—aimed at Sports Car Club of America (SCCA) Trans Am "sedan" road racing series competition—and a 325-hp 396-cid big-block V-8 in new SS 396 models. Only 602 '67 Z-28s were produced.

So with two different sixes and six V-8s, Camaro now could compete with anything in the fast-growing U.S. ponycar class, including Plymouth's new Barracuda, Mercury's Cougar (essentially a softer, plusher Mustang), and even GM's later-arriving Pontiac Firebird. In addition, according to Chevrolet records, a small (but unspecified) number of 375-hp 396 engines were delivered in '67 Camaros via special orders.

Camaro got off to a strong start in its debut year and jumped to a solid second in class. Given the Mustang's 2½-year head start and increasingly strong competition, '67 Camaro sales were a very respectable 201,134 versus Mustang's 442,686. An SS 350 paced the 1967 Indianapolis 500, and (despite GM's ban on factory participation) Camaro's Z-28—campaigned by Roger

This unassuming 1969 LeMans Blue coupe is one of the rarest and most exotic Camaros ever built. It's one of just 69 equipped with the awesome ZL1 V-8—an aluminum-head, aluminum-block 427. The ZL1 was factory-rated at 430 horsepower, but actual output was over 500. And it weighed just 500 pounds—about the same as Chevy's 327-cid V-8. The production ZL1 Camaros were built primarily to qualify the engine for NHRA racing, and were sparsely equipped—though the engine alone added a staggering $4160 to the sticker price.

Penske, with driver Mark Donohue, and some talented independents—scored three wins and finished third in points in the SCCA's Trans Am series.

Evolutionary engineering improvements and some cosmetic changes, including side marker lamps and a redesigned nose stripe, arrived for 1968. *Car and Driver* pushed a '68 Z-28 to a stunning 5.3-second 0-60 sprint, 13.8 seconds at 107 mph for the quarter-mile, and a 132 mph top end. Model-year sales improved to 217,700 (to Mustang's receding 299,061), and Donohue won the 1968 Trans Am series with a dominating 10 wins in Roger Penske's Sunoco Camaro.

Nineteen sixty-nine brought a bolder look and more refinement, plus new instruments and seats, an optional damage-resistant body-color front bumper, a regular-gas 250-hp 350 V-8 engine, an optional 3-speed Turbo Hydra-matic transmission, and a Hurst shifter for the 4-speed manual. A total of 69 1969 ZL1 Camaros (essentially de-striped Z-28s powered by Chevy's aluminum 427-cid drag-racing engine) were built and are prized collectibles today. A Z-28 paced that year's Indy 500, and Penske/Donohue took the Trans Am title again. But sales slipped to 193,986, about 100,000 fewer than Mustang, in an increasingly crowded ponycar market.

Opposite and above: By 1969, Don Yenko had found a better way to produce his 427 Super Camaros. By using Chevrolet's Central Office Production Order (or COPO) system, Yenko was able to order a limited run of Camaros with the L72 427 and other special equipment installed at the factory. His dealership would then apply Yenko stripes and badging (including "SYC" headrest logos). *This page:* Far out! The 1969 Camaro Berlinetta show car boasted wire wheels, special grille, trippy upholstery, under-dash stereo tuner, and a paint job in graduated shades of lavender.

SECOND GENERATION: PERSISTENCE PAYS OFF

The all-new second-generation Camaro was well worth the wait when it finally arrived late in February 1970. Tired of playing catch-up, Chevy set out to make it not just the best-yet Camaro but also a true four-seat sports car and the most beautiful Chevrolet ever designed.

The only body style was a semi-fastback coupe with a choice of two front ends. The standard face had a full-width bumper, the striking Rally Sport (RS) just two slim bumperettes flanking a protruding, slightly v-shaped grille opening with round parking lamps inboard of the headlamps. The otherwise unprotected RS grille was surrounded by a rim of damage-resistant body color urethane, and a slim, black-rubber protective rib ran vertically up its centerline. Around back, four round taillamps restored the Chevrolet family resemblance.

The look was part Jaguar, part Ferrari, all gorgeous. The Z28 boasted a new high-performance 360-hp 350 cid LT1 V-8, plus special suspension, larger wheels and tires, hood and decklid striping and a rear spoiler, and the RS appearance option could be paired with it, or with SS 350 or SS 396 equipment. But the real stories are in its design and engineering.

Exterior

"We started working on a new Camaro immediately after the '67 was announced," said then-Chevrolet General Manager (and GM Vice President) Pete Estes. "We worked really hard on the styling of that second one. We said it had to be the most beautiful automobile we have ever designed, and [GM Design Vice President] Bill Mitchell did the job. He had it in a special room, and nobody got in there except us. We wanted it to last like a Ferrari. There is no reason to change cars so often if you do the job right. I rarely went two days without being in that studio. Most of the good-looking cars at GM were done without too much 14th floor [cor-

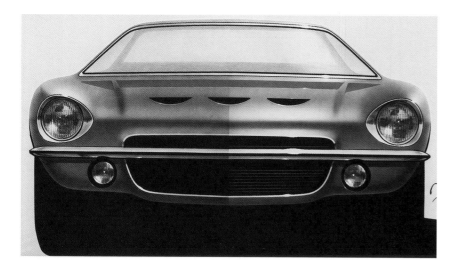

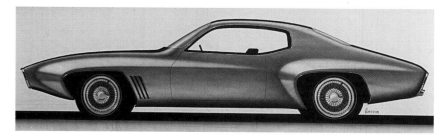

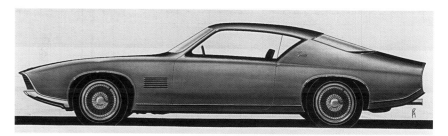

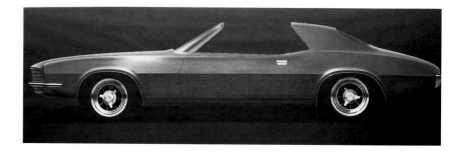

porate leadership] involvement, and we got this one done almost before they knew about it.

"We spent about 2½ months on the packaging, just getting the seats down, moving the frame out and working with the cross-section to get the proper anatomy. If you can package a car right, get the proportions—size of glass, thickness-of-body to length-of-hood and length-of-deck, the proper cross-section for the length and height of the vehicle—then you're going to get a good-looking piece regardless of what body configurations you use on the sheet metal. That was our basic premise on the '70½."

Mitchell added that Henry "Hank" Haga's studio designed the '70½ Camaro "really fast, with no interference. We were in the mood, and for some reason, nobody bothered us. We had started to separate the studios at that time, so it wasn't done alongside a Nova. We got the Camaro and the Corvette together, and the guys working on them were different types. All the pictures on their walls were race cars."

Dave Holls, Chevrolet Group Chief Designer at the time, remembers the second-generation Camaro program as, "Heaven, the most fun project I've ever been involved in. Everybody loved it and got excited about

1970 "F" DELUXE

Opposite: Stylists experimented with inset hood scoops, pronounced fender blisters, radical rooflines, half tops, and hidden windshield pillars in these design renderings. *This page:* The 1970½ Camaro dashboard wore a much-toned-down version of this sketch's wraparound design theme. Styling studies for the second-generation Camaro were underway as early as August 1966 (below). A pinched rear deck characterizes this example from September 1966 (left). Another study from the same period wore an evolution of the '69 Camaro grille.

it. The feeling was, 'Okay, we've answered the Mustang, but we haven't exceeded it. Now it's time to take the lead.' It was sort of, 'lock the doors and don't let anybody in here. We're going to do this one ourselves.'

"The most unique thing about it was development of the roof and windshield, without a rear quarter window. While that may not sound like much, it hadn't been done since the '36 Ford, or something. That gave it an intimate feeling and some tremendous advantages. We got rid of the cost of that quarter window and put the savings into other things we needed. We had to have a long door so we wouldn't have the big blind rear quarter, and that dictated a wraparound windshield. That windshield and the one-piece side window were key items in the architecture of the car."

Haga called it "very much a designer's car. It had the proportions, the dash-to-axle, and the low cowl, because it did not have to share any of these important elements with any other models. It was more of a shape car, not as much involved with looking like the widest architecture front and rear as it was with forms and tapered shapes that tucked in behind the rear wheels and in front of the front wheels. It became more wheel and tire accented and more masculine looking."

He added that most of the designers wanted to raise the level of detail and give the rear design a more aggressive look, but they were outvoted by some "corporate elders" who insisted that the rear should terminate in a slim horizontal loop. And inside that loop were two pairs of traditional

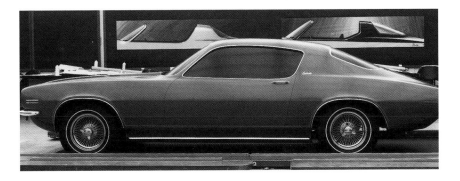

Opposite: Stylists had settled on the second-generation Camaro's smooth-sided "fuselage" body shape by late '67–early '68, but roof lines, window shapes, and front/rear fascia treatments were still in flux. Designers tried a variety of rear quarter-window arrangements before choosing to utilize very long doors with no quarter windows at all. This made for very large, heavy doors, but also saved on production costs; eliminating that extra piece of glass and its associated hardware freed up money that could be used in other areas of the car. *This page:* A side-profile view of a November 1967 clay model (top) shows angular quarter windows, thin bumpers, and a less-fluid roof-to-rear-deck transition. This Berlinetta-badged clay model (above) wears more-rounded window corners and other minor differences, but is otherwise very close to the final production car. Many different front-end treatments were tried; pictured at right are two that didn't make the final cut.

Chevrolet round taillamps. While they had wanted to get away from the Corvair look on the first-generation car, they decided that identification with the round-taillamp Corvette would be a good thing this time around.

And there was just one body style, a semi-fastback coupe with a roof that then-Chevrolet Chief Designer Irv Rybicki said, "just pours out onto the rear deck very easily." There was at one time a slick-looking convertible clay model in the studio, but the proposed production convertible was eventually dropped because it would have required a large additional tooling investment for a relatively small number of incremental sales.

Interior

As before, George Angersbach's Chevrolet #2 Interior Studio was charged with the responsibility of designing a new cockpit in keeping with the striking new exterior. "We felt that the '70½ was our opportunity to do the interior the way we really wanted it," Angersbach said. "And that was when we set up our studios, interior and exterior, next to one another. Being next door to Hank, it became sort of a family affair, and we really got rolling on that car."

Continued on page 54

As they had with the first-generation Camaro, designers tinkered with a two-door sport-wagon body style. Note the variations in these "Kammback" design studies—the hidden windshield pillars on the top two cars give the illusion of a cantilevered roof, while the bottom car's windshield area matches the production coupe. Neither wagon nor convertible body styles would ever find their way into showrooms; the second-generation Camaro was available only as a coupe for the entirety of its 1970-81 model-year run.

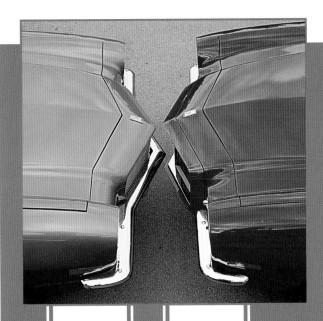

TWO FACES

Most agree that the '70^1/2 Camaro's frontal styling was a very key element in its overall appeal. Yet that Jaguar-inspired theme came along fairly late in the exterior design program.

"Initially the car carried a simple loop front end," said Chief Designer Henry Haga, "which evolved from the previous Camaro. But [GM Design Vice President Bill] Mitchell was not content with such an easy solution. He wanted a front end that had a much fresher and more distinct character."

At one point Mitchell returned from an overseas trip and blew his shiny top. "I came back from Europe one day," he said, "and they had a front on that car that could have been a Nova! I said, 'A sports car can't have the same kind of front on it as a regular passenger car!'

"I walked down the hall, and one of the pictures in the hall leading to my office showed a car [probably a Jaguar] with a front on it that really grabbed me. I said, 'Just take that off the wall and make it like that.' That's when we started getting the snaky fronts on the car."

The program moved along fairly quickly and smoothly after that as the frontal themes became dominated by large, low, mouth-like grille openings, as far as possible below the headlamp plane, and "catwalks" connecting the fenders and hood. Two different but related faces were designed: one with a full-width bumper and outboard parking lamps in the valence below it, the second with an open, unobstructed grille flanked by tiny bumperettes and round parking lamps in the catwalk between it and the headlamps.

Though favored by nearly everyone, this latter treatment—heavily influenced by the British Jaguar sedan of the time—had three strikes against it: 1) it would be expensive to manufacture, 2) it offered essentially no bumper protection, and 3) it required that the front license plate be mounted off-center, something Chevy's Corvette designers had never been allowed to do despite some cooling problems with a center-mounted plate.

"We had tried lots of ordinary fronts," Chevrolet Group Chief Designer Dave Holls said. "When we got to that one, it gave the car kind of an expensive look. All of a sudden, it looked like $1,000 more car! I never thought we would go with that more expensive version, with just a little rubber bar in the middle for protection. I thought at the last minute we would have a corporate review, and the more conservative element would say, 'We just can't do that, it's got no bumper.' Also, we really had a bind on cost. We had to have a base car that came in at the right price. But once we got that nose, that was key."

Surprisingly, Haga recalls no hassle over the offset license plate. "We wanted that," he said, "to save what became the Rally Sport front. We had two front ends going, and both looked great, and the impasse between the low-cost version and the alternate expensive proposal was resolved when one was selected for the base car and the other for the for the up-option model, which became the split-bumper, urethane nose RS version."

And once the less-expensive design became standard and the other an option, the cost of that beautiful optional RS version became much less of an issue.

—*Gary Witzenburg*

A profile shot of a 1970 Rally Sport shows the second-gen Camaro's clean, purposeful silhouette. The Z28 package was better than ever, thanks in part to the addition of a wonderful new 360-hp LT1 350. Suspension advances made all '70 Camaros good handlers, and the Z28, with firmer underpinnings and sticky Polyglas F60×15 tires, was a world class road car. The package's price tag jumped over $100 this year, to $572.95.

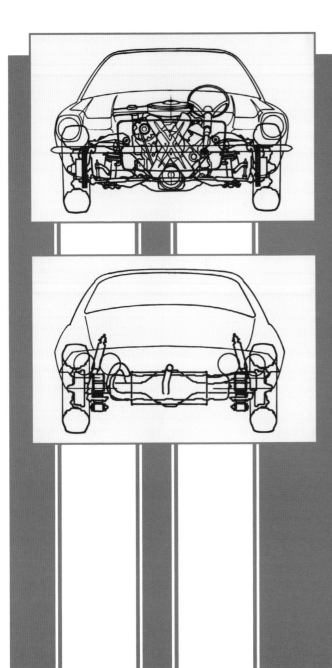

ADVANCED SUSPENSION

One key player responsible for re-engineering the Camaro from roof to tire patch was an up-and-coming young engineer named Bob Dorn. A former sports car racer who understood what a good handling car should be, he oversaw its chassis design and development.

One of the major chassis changes was moving the steering linkage from behind the front axles to a position in front of them, partially to provide better crash protection for the driver. "With a collapsible intermediate shaft," Dorn pointed out, "you can take up some of the crush without collapsing the steering column. We had to work on the steering ratio and the linkage to get the precise response we wanted.

"And when we went to the forward steer, we decided that the time was right to do a whole new front suspension for the corporation using integral cast knuckles with the caliber mounted directly to the knuckle. It would be the same thing that we would put into the next-generation full-size B-cars. We were trying to fit a 396 engine into the Camaro and at the same time use a corporate suspension with the longest possible upper and lower control arms to get the kind of ride that would satisfy Buick, Olds, and Pontiac for their B-cars.

"Then we looked at the rear suspension and found that adding more understeer actually made the car more precise, as long as we didn't add too much. We knew we were going to put large engines in the car, so we wanted to be sure to avoid some of the power problems we had with the previous car. We started with single leaf springs, but as the car got heavier, we had to go to higher-rate mono-plates to handle the wind-up conditions, and that made it ride more harshly than we wanted. We ended up having to go to multi-leafs to get the ride frequencies down where we wanted them, and it was during the long-lead-time magazine writers' preview out at Riverside Raceway, just a few months before public introduction, that we convinced [then Chevrolet General Manager] John DeLorean that we ought to put multi-leaf springs on all Camaros rather than just the high-performance versions.

"When we built all that into the car, it turned out to be a whiz-bang, just fantastic! We didn't have the axle control problems we'd anticipated, and we had just the right amount of understeer. You could do anything with it, go down the road and toss it sideways. The car was super forgiving. It tracked straight down the road with good on-center feel and without a lot of wind wander. The front suspension was complemented by a rear suspension with enough understeer built in that it didn't try to steer the car during cornering. Some cars tend to steer the driver, but that Camaro was designed so the driver could do what he wanted with it without getting into trouble. I think the car had more ability than all but the best drivers could use."

An optional F41 handling package, developed around the softer-rate base springs, included heavy-duty shock absorbers and—computer tuned for each engine/tire combination—a rear stabilizer bar and a larger front bar. Much-improved stopping power was provided by standard manual front disc brakes with new-design integral cast hub/rotors.

—Gary Witzenburg

SS models rounded out Camaro's performance lineup for 1970. The SS 350 featured a tamer 300-hp 350, but the rarely seen SS 396 was offered in 350- and, by special order, 375-hp versions of Chevy's "big block" V-8, which at this point actually displaced 402 cubic inches. This Shadow Gray SS 350 is equipped with the $168.55 Rally Sport option package, which included a distinctive split-bumper nose and round parking lamps. The rear deck spoiler tacked on another $32.65.

Continued from page 51

With the objective of making the new interior much more innovative, sporty, and driver-oriented than the previous one, the design team as early as mid-1967 began cranking out some very revolutionary concepts, most with instrument clusters isolated from the passenger side and wrapping around into the driver-side door panel. As these were translated into life-size mockups in seating bucks and became more practical and less expensive to manufacture, the wraparound idea was retained. The final result, with large central speedometer and tachometer flanked by twin pairs of smaller round gauges and with lighting, wipers, and accessory switches outboard of them, was exciting, attractive, and highly usable.

Engineering

Any new-car design so dominated by styling is bound to cause problems for engineers, and Holls related that one day, when the styling was essen-

TOUGH TRANS AM

The SCCA's Trans Am series reached a spectacular crescendo of excitement in 1970. Riding the crest of a popularity wave that had drawn over 224,000 spectators to 13 events the previous year, it enjoyed an unprecedented surge of factory interest and money.

Unfortunately, American Motors had pulled off a shocking surprise: stealing Roger Penske and company from Chevrolet. If anyone could make the Javelin a winning race car (and maybe a serious ponycar player) to crush the "grandmother Rambler" image, America's smallest automaker figured, Penske and engineer/driver Mark Donohue could.

Penske predicted that his new Javelin team would take seven victories and the title. AMC marketing Vice President Bill McNealy added, "It's going to be a hand-to-hand struggle among the behemoths of Detroit, and AMC is going to be top dog with proven winners."

Chevrolet, with its stunningly styled new '70½ Camaros but without the team that had brought it 21 wins and two straight titles in three seasons, hired ace-Can Am racing series technology wizard Jim Hall, whose Chaparral Camaros would be piloted, at one time or another, by Ed Leslie, Vic Elford, Joe Leonard, and Hall himself. There was also an Owens Corning Camaro team of Tony DeLorenzo and Jerry Thompson, fresh off an SCCA A-Production big-bore Corvette National Championship, plus some other strong independents.

Ford was counting on its high-dollar Bud Moore Mustang effort with Parnelli Jones and George Follmer. Pontiac had Jerry Titus and Craig Fisher, and AMC had Peter Revson backing up Donohue. There was a new Plymouth Barracuda fielded by Dan Gurney for talented up-and-comer Swede Savage and an all-new Dodge Challenger for Sam Posey, plus another car for each team supposedly in the works. It would be the most formidable field of well-financed cars and talent for any American production-based road racing series ever.

And when the dust and tire smoke settled, the championship belonged to Ford with six wins, five from Jones and one from Follmer. The Penske Javelins suffered early teething troubles, but Donohue took a trio of victories and enough points to bring AMC a respectable second place (again!). Pontiac had a terrible and tragic year, scoring zero points and losing Jerry Titus in the early series' only fatal accident. And while the Dodge and Plymouth cars went well at times, mechanical troubles kept them out of the winner's circle.

With all four U.S. makers involved, without Penske/Donohue and with its racing budget severely cut due to recession, Chevrolet took just two wins and third in points. Elford scored one for the Chaparral team and Milt Minter another in his independent Camaro. A disappointing finish, it would mark the end of GM factory involvement for many years.

—*Gary Witzenburg*

tially complete and the models sitting in a hallway at Design Staff, Mitchell called his team down and asked, "'Okay, that's it. Are you guys happy?' We said, 'Yes sir!' And he said, 'Okay then, don't let anybody screw it up!' And, believe me, it was a struggle to get that car made."

"We said that this second Camaro has to be the ultimate, a baby Corvette," Estes related. "We put our best chassis guys on it and made it lower, cheated the inside room as tight as we could, put a new stub frame under it, changed the front suspension, improved the rear suspension and widened the tread."

One major engineering challenge was designing the underbody stamping to get the car as low as it was. "The stretches and contortions that had

Top left: The 1970 "Landau" show car was built for singer Glen Campbell. The Landau's targa-style roof predicted Camaro's T-bar roof option, which would arrive much later. *Left:* The nose of the 1971 XP-888 GT two-seat concept car shows more exotic European influence. *Above:* Partly because of the short 1970 model run, changes for 1971 Camaros were minor: high-back bucket seats, plus a cushioned-center steering wheel on Sport Coupe and RS models and a new sport steering wheel for the SS and Z28. Engines were detuned to run on low-lead gas, and hp ratings were reported in more-realistic net figures instead of gross numbers. *Opposite:* The Z28, now rated at 275 horsepower net and with lowered compression, watched output plummet from 8733 units in 1970 to 4862 for '71.

The 1972 A/F Coupe styling study made a number of unconventional design alterations to the Camaro's basic shape—none of which were particularly predictive of future production-Camaro styling. Among the A/F Coupe's unique features were grille-mounted inboard headlights, a tapered fastback roofline with large rear-quarter windows, and a sloped rear-end with thin horizontal taillights.

An optional "wet-look" vinyl top was one of a handful of minor changes to the 1972 Camaro. The big-block "396" was down to 240 horsepower, and would disappear altogether after this year. A crippling strike at Camaro's sole assembly plant in Norwood, Ohio, resulted in drastically lower model-year production of 68,656 units. With that, GM executives strongly considered dumping the Camaro, but thankfully they never dropped the axe.

to be made on that underbody were unbelievable," Holls said. Another was the low cowl. "We had problems with packaging the cowl," Rybicki added. "We wanted it as low as we could get it because we were forcing the roof down much lower than the original car's. When we got into it with the engineers, they gave us a bad time about the cowl. They wanted to raise it an inch to an inch and a half to get more room for packaging the air-conditioning, instrumentation and so forth. I can remember fighting the Chevrolet group for months. It was a standoff, and time was getting short.

"That is the crucial line in the automobile; the base of the windshield and where it is positioned sets up everything—height of windshield, height of car, sightlines out over the hood, where you place the driver. I had to get Mitchell into the studio one day, and in his inimitable fashion, he gave them a speech they wouldn't forget for a while. And then we got the cowl where we wanted it. But we were not interfered with at all in interior packaging."

This page: After another round of minor changes for 1973, the '74 Camaro sported new stronger front and rear spring-mounted aluminum bumpers with resilient impact strips, redesigned grille, and "sugar scoop" headlights and parking lights. Federally-mandated five-mph crash regulations meant that the split-bumper RS nose was history. *Opposite:* The sporty Z28 was powered by a solid-lifter 245-horsepower 350. Bold hood and decklid stripes were a $77 option that was not for bashful types; about half of the 13,802 Z28s built for '74 got them. The Z28 would go on a brief hiatus after 1974, returning as a separate model midway through the 1977 model year.

Promoted to director of engineering in 1966, Alex Maier had gotten into the first Camaro's development late in the game, but he was heavily involved in the second generation from the very beginning. And he was determined that it was going to be better in every way than the 1967-69, as well as the competition. "We viewed the '70½ car as a nice opportunity to do it over again," he recalled, "and this time, we were not trying to catch up; we were looking for leadership." This meant much-improved handling and braking in addition to better styling inside and out, whether or not it created difficulties for his engineers.

"We looked heavily into the design," he added, "and Henry Haga had a free hand on it. We had to do new manifolds and carburetors and air cleaners to get under his hood, but we did them. We knew we were not going to do any convertibles, so we didn't have to do the job of working out the shake. We did look at whether we needed both a notchback and a fastback, but Henry's group did an outstanding job [on the roofline] that surprised everyone. It was neither a fastback nor a notchback but kind of

Opposite and left: The most noticeable change for 1975 Camaros was a larger wraparound rear window that improved rear vision. Like many '75 Detroit cars, Camaro engines adopted catalytic converters that permitted cleaner exhaust and improved drivability on the required unleaded gasoline. Just three engine choices were offered: a 105-hp 250 six, a 145-hp 350 V-8, and a 155-hp 350. *Below:* The 1976 Rally Sport package didn't include any real performance upgrades, but definitely grabbed eyes with its satin-black two-tone paint treatment, tri-color striping and logos, and body-color-matched wheels.

a semi-fastback that appealed to both groups. We felt comfortable that we didn't need anything else."

One battle the engineers did win over the stylists involved the car's stance. The original Camaro had been trimmed with its rear end slightly higher than its front, and because it was designed around small tires, it sat too high on larger tires. That prompted management to drop it down, which eliminated much of its ride travel. In doing the second-gen suspension, lead engineer Bob Dorn's chassis group actually gave it ³/₈-inch *downward* rake at the back to avoid repeating the ride-height/travel problem.

This stance may not have been as good aesthetically, but with plenty of suspension travel (three inches of jounce at four-passenger load), big-car chassis componentry, and better isolation, the re-engineered Camaro

rode far more softly and smoothly than its predecessors. It was also more comfortable inside with redesigned seats, increased front-seat travel, extended front and rear legroom, and five inches additional rear-seat entry room because of its long doors—though the rear-seat area was still cramped for adults.

Another substantial improvement was in sound insulation. Instead of piling on heavy, expensive sound-deadening materials, the engineers acoustically tuned the entire body to eliminate unwanted noise and vibrations from the passenger compartment. Sound barriers and improved body-seam sealing blocked openings where drivetrain and road noises might have intruded. New "trapped-edge" wind seals around the side windows eliminated nearly all wind noise at speed, and a special double-roof design —a perforated inner panel and vinyl headliner over a sound-absorbing blanket—soaked up most of what noise did get inside.

Because both designers and engineers were determined to do the job

100 percent right this time, the development process took longer than anticipated. And when the car was not ready for a summer 1969 production startup and a traditional fall launch, it was reluctantly decided to delay it a full year, make it a '71 model and continue the '69 unchanged as the '70. But the final decision was to launch the new Camaro as a '70 as soon as it was ready—which turned out to be February 26, 1970—and continue building '69 models for a few extra months.

The Launch

When the stunning new Camaro finally did hit the street, *Car and Driver* magazine said it was "the first of a new generation of American GT cars— low, taut and sleek of flank . . .a blend of agility, comfort and silence beyond anything the world has ever seen in a GT car of this price . . . Its shape is smoother than any Detroit effort we can think of . . . The new instrument panel is a brilliant layout, but it still gives the feeling of a posh tourer rather

Opposite: Other than newly optional intermittent wipers and the return of the Z28, the 1977 Camaro was a virtual rerun of the '76 line-up. *This page:* For 1978, the eight-year-old Camaro body got its second and final major facelift. Body-color, energy-absorbing front and rear bumpers, larger taillights, and plusher optional interiors were among the changes. New car shoppers approved, and Camaro sales grew to a record 247,437 units for the year. Chevrolet had another reason to celebrate on May 11, 1978, when the two-millionth Camaro was built.

than a taut GT car . . . The driving position is extremely good, and the interior is far more spacious, particularly in the rear seat area, than you would expect in a fastback." *Car and Driver* tested a '70 Z-28 at 5.8 seconds 0-60 mph, 14.2 seconds in the quarter-mile, and a 118 mph top speed. And rival *Road & Track* went so far as to call it "the best American car . . . and more importantly . . . one of the most satisfying cars for all-around use, we've ever driven."

Opposite: The 1978 Z28 was little changed mechanically, but gained more flash via nonfunctional front-fender vents and a hood scoop. "It'll put butterflies in your stomach, a lump in your throat, and a smile on your face," proclaimed one ad. *This page:* "T-Top" removable roof panels, as seen on this Rally Sport, were a new and popular option for 1978 Camaros. Despite a midyear introduction and a stiff $625 retail price, 9875 '78 Camaros got them.

It was longer, lower, wider, and roomier than its predecessor, and just a partial list of its engineering, comfort, and convenience improvements included much-improved interior, seats, acoustics, and ventilation, stronger front subframe, wider treads, vastly improved suspension and brakes (with standard front discs), E78×14 bias-belted tires, optional variable-ratio power steering, and substantially softer ride. A 300-hp 350 cid V-8 was standard with the SS package, a 350-hp 396 was optional, and a few 375-horse 396s were available on a limited basis.

Showroom success came swiftly, and by April Camaro zoomed past Mustang in monthly sales. However, due to its lateness to market—and because the whole "sport compact" class had begun losing favor with buyers—1970 model-year results were unspectacular at 148,301, second-in-class to Mustang's 170,003.

Opposite: For 1979, the Z28 got an air dam with integral front fender "spats" and bolder stripes. Base price jumped from $5604 to $6748, but buyers didn't seem to mind—production jumped to over 80,000, an increase of over 30,000 from 1978. This example wears the optional 15×7 "turbine" aluminum wheels, which were available only in '78 and '79. *This page:* All 1979 Camaros got a redesigned instrument cluster—tooling for the 1970-design panel had worn out. A new and very popular addition to the line this year was the luxury-level Berlinetta. This high-style Camaro replaced the Type LT, and included aluminum wheels and dual pinstripes.

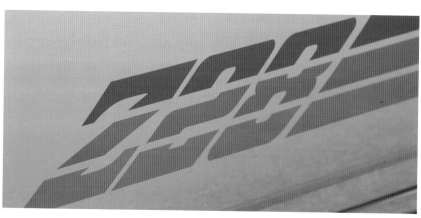

This page: Z28s received another round of striping and trim revisions for 1980, including a new body-color vertical-bar grille, functional front-fender vents, and rear-wheel well fender flares. A new "air induction" rear-facing hood scoop used a solenoid-activated intake door that opened at full throttle to draw cool air to the carburetor. The standard 190-hp 350 V-8 was good for 0-60 mph in about 9.5 seconds. *Opposite:* Non-Z28 Camaros offered an efficient base 229 V-6 with 115 horsepower, replacing the old inline 250, and economy-tune 267- and 305-cid V-8s with 125 and 155 hp, respectively. Ritzy Berlinetta models now came standard with faux wire wheelcovers. At $6606, the Berlinetta was priced in between the $5843 base sport coupe and the top-of-the-line Z28, which retailed for $7363.

Evolutionary Change

Gen II Camaros changed little through the early 1970s except to accommodate new safety and emissions standards. A luxury LT model arrived for '73; new fascias with beefed-up bumpers accompanied federal bumper rules for '74 while, sadly, the Z28 was dropped for '75 in the wake of 1973's fuel crisis. Following a low of just 70,809 '72 models, sales recovered and climbed steadily to 91,678 '73s, 135,780 '74s, 135,102 '75s and 163,653 '76s, nearly matching the (downsized for '74) Mustang's 178,541.

As the sporty car market and Camaro demand slowly recovered, Chevy decided to re-launch the Z28 in mid-'77. Then-Chevrolet General Manager Bob Lund called it a "driver's car" and maybe "the best-handling production vehicle ever built." Powered by a 350-cid V-8 rated at 170 hp (under the conservative SAE rating system introduced—along with catalytic converters, unleaded gas, and heavy emission con-

trols—for 1971), it featured special steering and suspension tuning and GR70×15 radial tires on 15×7-inch wheels. Not surprisingly, Camaro finally outsold Mustang that year with sales of 198,755 to 161,654.

New body-color bumpers freshened the look for '78, a luxury Berlinetta model replaced the LT for '79, and a more fuel-efficient V-6 replaced the straight six for '80. Model-year sales peaked at 247,437 '78s

and 233,802 '79s, then fell again to 131,066 '80s following a second fuel crisis in 1979. In its final calendar year, Camaro sales (including some new Gen III '82s) totaled just 94,606. After a fine decade-long run, the stage was set for Chevy's beautiful Gen II Camaro to be replaced by an even better and more exciting all-new generation.

Opposite: The aging Camaro fought one last round for 1981, setting a new GM longevity record for the styling of a high-volume car. The Rally Sport model was dropped, power brakes and a Space Saver spare tire became standard on all models, and halogen headlights were offered. Total Camaro sales fell 17 percent to 126,139. Just 20,253 of those were Berlinettas. *This page:* The Z28 soldiered into 1981 with little change. The five-spoke aluminum wheels seen here were optional on any '81 Camaro.

Amid late-Seventies doubts about the prospects for the "ponycar" market in general, Chevrolet began planning for a new generation of its Camaro. The car it came up with proved to be tougher than the odds.

THIRD GENERATION: THE WILL TO SURVIVE

Given the sagging fortunes of American ponycars in general during the Seventies, it's a wonder that GM persevered to design and develop a brand-new Camaro. The evolution of a new Camaro/Firebird "F-car" design, originally intended as a 1980 model, began early in 1975 in Bill Porter's Advanced Studio and Jerry Palmer's Chevrolet Studio. Believe it or not, they were seen at first as front-drive sporty coupes spun off the new compact X-cars being developed for the '80 model year—logical, considering that space- and fuel-efficient front-wheel drive was the industry's direction at the time, and the F-cars had always been derivatives of compact family cars.

A Change in Plans

By March 1977, the initial designs were nearly ready for release, but production plans had been moved back to 1981. Then GM Design Vice President Bill Mitchell retired, replaced on August 1 by Irv Rybicki, who made a review of every ongoing program. Among other things, he ordered a Camaro/Firebird redirection. As a result, in January 1978, Porter's studio was ordered to start again on the third-generation F-cars, which were now scheduled as '82 models.

"[Porter] had an assistant . . . by the name of Roger Hughet [who] turned out an illustration," Rybicki recalled around the time of the car's introduction. "We took one look at it and . . . said, 'Do it in scale.' Then we tried it full-size, and it was a success from the very beginning. We didn't think we could get there because this car is considerably shorter and narrower, has better seating in back, a hatch, and fold-down rear seats. And we've got one design feature on it that no one else has ever done. We take the backlight glass and form it into a compound curve in two directions, and then it flows right into the sheetmetal surfaces. There is a deck, but you never quite see the break."

By May, Palmer's Chevrolet studio was back into the project. "At that

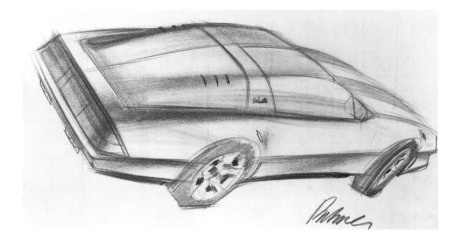

time," he said, "it was back to rear-wheel drive. The package had been settled, the wheelbase and the interior dimensions. We had all the dots to connect now, and the more we got into it, the better it got . . . and we were fighting for a 'faster' windshield, a 62-degree windshield. By July, we had a pretty serious model . . . and we were pretty proud of it."

Creation of the new F-car interiors began in fall 1977, shortly after Rybicki took over as styling chief, in a new concept interior studio under John Shettler. "We started to study the Lear business jets and the Concorde, which have tremendous aerodynamics," Shettler recalled. "Their windshields are pushed down almost flat, and they have these big hoods over the instruments to cut down glare and reflections. We decided to get the feel of those hoods, to bring the controls, and the gauges, and all the parts that might reflect in the windshield pulled back toward the driver."

Engineering Concept

Camaro chief engineer Tom Zimmer's group had begun formulating the next-generation's engineering concept late in 1976. "In gross terms," he recalled, "the objectives were to significantly reduce the weight of the car;

try to keep the seating for the front passengers essentially unchanged; improve, or at least maintain, the rear seating; significantly improve the luggage capacity; maintain a specialty-car character, high-styled with a sporty image; and improve the fuel economy. We felt we knew going in what the mission of this car ought to be. It ought to be an extremely good-handling car. . . . [W]e used benchmarks like the Lotus Esprit and the Porsche 924."

In June 1977, the new F-car became a GM corporate Engineering Staff project led by project manager Bob Knickerbocker. "We started in a very preliminary way putting together the various proposals that would produce a 1982 car in the Camaro and Firebird image," he related. "At that time, we examined the many options that were available: front-wheel drive, rear-wheel drive, two-passenger cars, four-passenger cars, different powertrains, and different concepts of fuel economy and performance. As it turned out, the concept was a rear-wheel-drive car with a significant spectrum of powertrains that would provide good fuel economy on one end and reasonable performance, but with improved fuel economy over 1981, on the other . . . [and] a four-passenger car, because the rear seat in an F-car is still a very usable thing, even though it's been bad-mouthed by a lot of people in the past."

Opposite: Undated sketches by Jerry Palmer (left) and John Cafaro (right) capture many of the elements of the third-generation Camaro. *This page, above:* A prominent above-bumper grille and rear-bumper exhaust cutouts were under consideration in August 1978. *Below:* The 1982 Camaros rode a much-improved chassis with front MacPherson struts and lower control arms replacing dual A-arms, rear coil springs instead of leafs, and a torque tube to better locate the live rear axle. Disc brakes were optional across the board. This "phantom" view also highlights the new hatch rear window that lifted up for access to greatly increased luggage space.

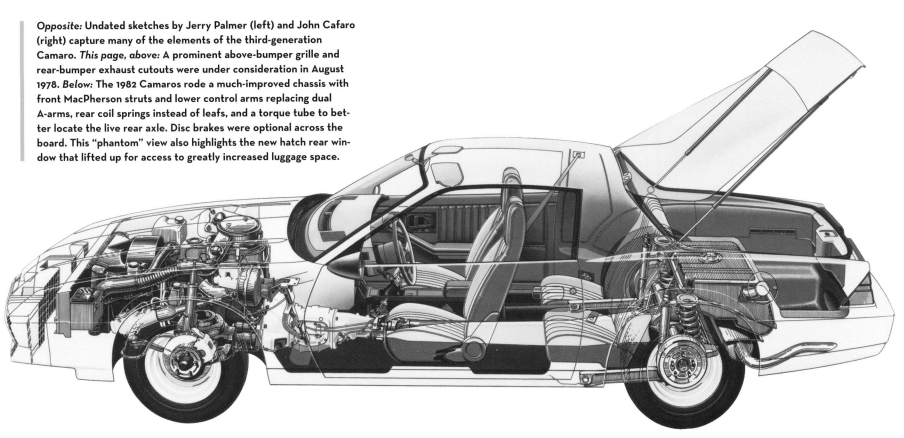

Added Zimmer, "In spite of the obvious trend to front-wheel drive, when we aligned our priorities and looked at the customer and the market we were trying to serve, the facilities, the packaging, the mass, the fuel economy, and all those things, and looked at what kind of physical arrangement would produce the kind of car we wanted, we said we wanted to make it rear-wheel drive."

The Launch

The all-new third-generation 1982 Camaro debuted with great fanfare to an excitement-starved American market. In Z28 form, it graced the covers of nearly every auto magazine, paced that year's Indianapolis 500, and was named "Car of the Year" by *Motor Trend*. "Our engineers are excited by what they were able to accomplish with the 1982 Camaro," then-Chevrolet Chief Engineer Paul King enthused. "We've made the best better."

For the first time, a four-cylinder engine—a 2.5-liter throttle-body fuel-injected unit rated at 90 hp—powered the base sport coupe. Chevy said that, when coupled to the standard four-speed manual transmission, the inline four performed about as well as the larger, heavier base V-6 that powered the '81 Camaro while delivering 20 percent better fuel economy. Optional engines were a 102-hp 2.8-liter two-barrel-carbureted V-6 and a 145-horse 5.0-liter four-barrel V-8. These last two powerplants were

Opposite: A 1982 Z28, still Camaro's performance leader, fronts its second-generation predecessor. The new car was 7 inches shorter, 3 inches slimmer, and fractionally lower on a new 104-inch wheelbase. *This page, top:* Designers aimed to give the '82 Camaro an all-new look while continuing certain identifying styling cues such as single side windows, wide rear roof pillars, and broad tri-color taillights. *Bottom:* The racy Z28 priced from $9700 and tallied 63,563 sales. *Motor Trend* awarded the new Camaro lineup its 1982 Car of the Year award.

standard in the cushy Berlinetta and racy Z28 models, respectively. Outside of California, where emissions standards were more stringent, Z28 buyers hungrier for more go could select a throttle-body "Cross-Fire Injection" version of the 305-cid small-block V-8 rated at 165 hp and available (at first) with automatic transmission only. The other three engines could be teamed with either a four-speed manual or a three-speed automatic transmission.

Though smaller and lighter than its predecessor (wheelbase was shorter by seven inches and overall length was cut by almost ten inches), this new unibody Camaro lost little in interior room. The compound S-curve glass rear hatch provided easy cargo access, and a new advanced bumper design used honeycomb composite energy absorbers backed by high-strength steel or aluminum (depending on equipment levels) impact bars front and rear. The Z28 sported a front air dam integrated with flared rocker panels and a sheet-molded plastic hood with computer-controlled fresh-air intakes for the Cross-Fire V-8.

Inside, a standard center console contained the glovebox (the cutaway instrument panel design left no room for one in the dash), plus radio and climate controls, and a parking brake lever. The rear seatback folded down to expand cargo capacity, and a terrific "Conteur" driver seat with six separate adjustments—including thigh and lumbar supports—was optional in the Z28.

The new front suspension used MacPherson struts in place of the previous upper control arms and conventional shock absorbers, while coil

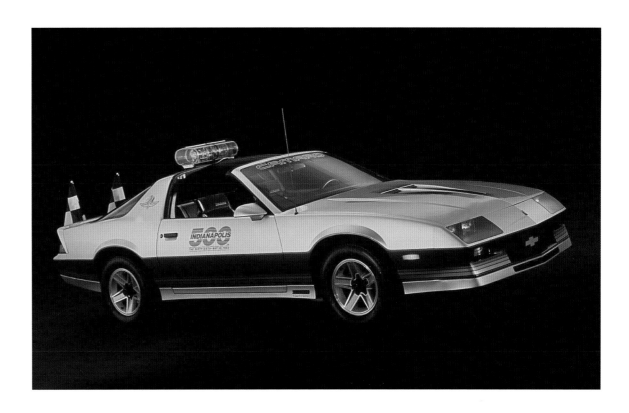

Opposite: **The Berlinetta continued as the posh Camaro. Its $9766 base price included V-6 power, aluminum wheels, an upgraded interior, and specific trim. Berlinetta shared its three-slot front fascia with base Camaros; Z28s wore a unique smooth nose.** *This page:* **Camaro was chosen as pace car for the 1982 Indy 500, its third such honor. Chevy celebrated by building 6360 replicas. All were specially trimmed silver and blue T-top Z28s, minus the roof light bar on the actual pacer (shown).**

springs replaced the old leaf springs in a new torque-arm arrangement in back and a track bar provided good lateral axle control. Though the new body was 2.7 inches narrower, the front tread was a mere half-inch less while the rear tread was up to an inch-and-a-half wider than in '81. The base sport coupe rolled on fiberglass-belted tires around 14×6 steel wheels, the Berlinetta got steel-belted radials on 14×7 gold-toned aluminum wheels, and the Z28 wore Goodyear Eagle GT performance radials on 15×7 five-spoke cast-aluminum wheels. Front disc brakes were standard; four-wheel discs were available for cars with V-8s.

Positive Press

Magazine reviews, most focusing on the Z28, were highly enthusiastic. While some complained that the Cross-Fire engine didn't quite get the performance job done, especially with no available manual transmission, all praised its styling and handling. "Initial one-word reviews . . . ran the gamut from 'Wow!' and 'Hot!' to 'Brilante!,'" wrote *Motor Trend*'s Tony Swan. "And based on this [January 1982] preview test, we're willing to call this piece—as well as its upstream sister at Pontiac—the best-handling car made in this country." Swan deemed the interior "tasteful, appealing," then summed up: "This new Z28 may not possess the sheer light-the-tires thrust of some of its predecessors from the age of big-block excess, but for our money it's better in every other measurement you'd care to name."

"It's lighter, it's smaller. Gas mileage is much improved. The new Z28 has superb seats and some of the stickiest tires money can buy. The handling is a take-home Bondurant course," wrote *Car and Driver*'s Don Sherman. "The body is so gorgeous, grown men will blush." Though Sherman raked the Z28's "crude" three-speed automatic, "lame" 5000-rpm redline, and "measly" 165 horsepower, his instrumented tests yielded 0-60 mph acceleration of 7.9 seconds, fairly respectable for 1982.

Your author was also duly impressed by the new Z28 (and its Pontiac Trans Am sister ship) when reporting on the F-cars in the February 1982 issue of *Popular Mechanics*. "We can tell you categorically that these cars

are nothing short of phenomenal in cornering power and overall handling
. . . and the standard suspension setups allow the other new Camaros and
Firebirds to acquit themselves surprisingly well, too," I wrote. "If you want
heart-stopping handling, enough power to spin the rear wheels at will, and
looks that will stop nubile young things in their tracks, look no further."

The Z28 handily won the *Motor Trend* Car of the Year Award over an
11-car field that *MT* called its finest ever. "It's a bold move, committing to
an all-new performance machine when everyone else is thinking economy," the article said. "The new Camaro boasts what is likely the most care-
fully developed 'handling' chassis ever issued by Detroit, as well as daring
sheet metal. The Z28 is the hard-core Camaro, offering proper suspension, 4-wheel discs, big tires and quick steering. Recaro-like support comes
from the excellent new Conteur driver's seat." It was the favorite of five

Opposite, top: For 1983, a high-output
(H.O.) 305 V-8 with a four-barrel carburetor was available as a late-season
option; net horsepower was rated at 190.
Bottom: The Z28's optional "Conteur"
seats boasted lumbar and thigh support adjusters similar to those of the
well-known Recaro buckets. *This page,
left:* Third-generation Camaro demand
peaked in 1984, a year in which Z28
production topped 100,000. *Above:*
Designers drew inspiration from
Learjet control panels when creating
the Camaro's dashboard.

of the six judges. "If you're making up your personal shopping list of great road cars and you don't have a Z28 or Trans Am on it, you need a new list," Swan opined. "The Camaro is simply the best American road car ever built," added Jim Hall. "When one car can meld supreme roadworthiness, dramatic styling and contemporary engineering in an exciting package that sells for $10,000, it deserves unique recognition," the story concluded.

Evolutionary Change

The following year brought new transmissions: a five-speed manual optional in the base Camaro, but standard on Z28 and Berlinetta; and a four-speed overdrive automatic available for all V-8-powered cars. Horsepower was nudged up in all '83 Camaro engines. Late in the model year, a 190-hp high-output four-barrel V-8 with a hotter cam and higher compression

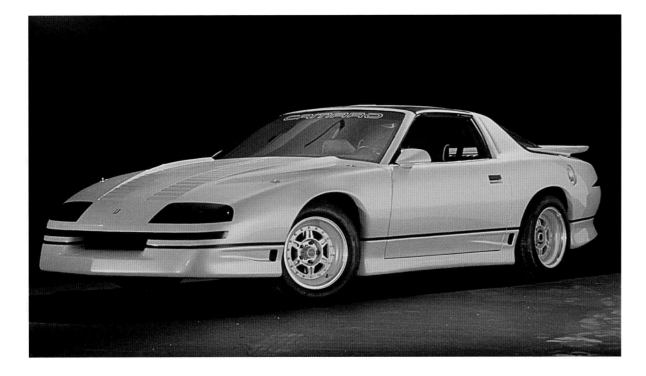

Opposite, top and left: The International Race of Champions drivers competition inspired the new IROC-Z. It featured a special front fascia, "ground effects" body skirts, and distinctive 16-inch cast-aluminum wheels. *Opposite right:* With the arrival of the IROC-Z, the "ordinary" Z28 was no longer top dog of the Camaro lineup. However, it could still be had with the top-of-the-line Camaro engine: a new port-injected 5.0 V-8 making a strong 215 hp. *This page:* Built to explore design ideas for future Camaros, the pearl-yellow GTZ concept car toured various auto shows in 1985. Underneath the radically louvered hood was a high-performance 4.3-liter V6.

Right: A base 1986 Camaro Sport Coupe started at $8935 with four-cylinder power. *Below:* Berlinettas were discontinued midyear due to slumping sales (just 4479 were built for '86), but the hot IROC-Z more than doubled its volume to 49,585. To meet federal regulations, all Camaros were equipped with a center high-mounted stop lamp (CHMSL) at the top of the hatchback window.

replaced the Cross-Fire engine as a Z28 option. A flashy "tri-tone" interior with the optional Conteur seat was another new extra-cost item for Z28s.

The Berlinetta moved upmarket for '84 with a "space-age" instrument panel with digital speedometer, vertical-bar tachometer, and adjustable control pods that brought key controls (lights and turn signals on the left, wipers and climate on the right) within fingertip reach of the steering wheel. An electronic stereo radio swiveled on a pedestal extending from the floor console, while a first-ever overhead console (optional on all other Camaros) contained the dome light, a map light, a storage pouch, and even a flashlight—batteries included.

"The Berlinetta is intended to be the 'mature' Camaro," wrote *Motor Trend*'s Jim Hall in a May 1984 review, "hence Chevy's engineers have smoothed out the F-car suspension. . . . The soft ride has been tuned to keep road noise, as well as harshness, to a minimum." On the downside, Hall added, "the Berlinetta lacks the fighter-plane reflexes of the Z28." *MT*

clocked a Berlinetta with a V-8 and four-speed automatic transmission (the three-speed no longer available for Camaros) at 9.25 seconds 0-60 mph and 16.99 seconds at 81.10 mph in the quarter-mile. Berlinetta sales perked up a bit, but not nearly as much as the base and Z28 models in what would prove to be the biggest model year for the third-generation Camaro.

For 1985, the V-6 got multiport fuel injection and other upgrades that raised its output from 107 to 135 hp. There were now three 5.0-liter V-8 choices: the standard Z28 mill, now rated at 155 hp; the 190-horse high-output carbureted job; and a new 215-hp tuned-port electronic fuel injection (TPI) option.

The best news of all was a hot new IROC package for the Z28, commemorating the International Race of Champions series, which featured some of the world's best drivers competing in identically prepared Camaros. Fitted with deep "ground effects" body cladding, chassis enhancements, and 16×8 alloy wheels, IROCs came with a choice of the high-output four-barrel V-8 with five-speed manual or the new TPI engine

Included in the $659 IROC-Z package were low-profile tires on handsome 16-inch wheels, special suspension, fog lights, and unique body graphics. A five-speed stick-shift replaced the four-speed as the new standard transmission for all Camaros. Following a trial with a pre-production '86 IROC-Z and an equivalent Mustang, *Hot Rod* magazine ranked Camaro as "still the best handling production sport coupe in America."

Opposite: Several aftermarket companies offered rear-window louvers for the Camaro's large hatchback glass. Chevrolet began offering its own version in 1986 as a $210 option. Lack of a callout beneath the Z28 emblem indicates that this IROC is not equipped with a fuel-injected engine; instead, it packs the carbureted 190-hp "high-output" 5.0-liter. *This page, left:* A 225-hp 5.7-liter TPI V-8 became optional in 1987 IROC-Zs. Performance with the muscular new motor was blistering for the day: 0-60 mph in under 6.5 seconds, the standing quarter-mile in less than 14.5 seconds at around 95 mph. *Below:* This 1987 Camaro family portrait includes a red IROC-Z, blue Z28, and two base Camaros. Unhappily for Chevy, total Camaro sales dropped 28.3 percent to 137,760.

with four-speed automatic. (The latter was also an option for the Z28.) "The '85 IROC-Z is a responsive, precise, hard-cornering weapon that will humble many Euro/Japanese cars sporting much fancier window stickers," Ron Grable wrote in *Motor Trend*. Zero-to-60 was measured at an impressive 6.87 seconds, the quarter-mile at 15.3 seconds at 89.1 mph, and skid-pad grip at a neck-straining 0.85g.

For 1986, the five-speed stickshift replaced the four-speed as the new standard transmission. Base coupes got a little sportier looking via standard styled steel wheels with trim rings and black lower-body

Continued on page 95

This page: Camaro turned 20 in 1987, and Chevy celebrated with the first Camaro convertible in 18 years. Available in any trim level, the revived ragtop was a factory-approved conversion by ASC Incorporated, which built just 1007 this season. At left, Livonia, Michigan, dealer Kit Tennyson (at wheel) takes delivery of the very first one from ASC executives John Hart (standing) and Mike Alexander. *Opposite:* An RS (Rally Sport) Camaro became available as a California-only option early in 1987. Built at Chevy's Van Nuys Camaro plant near Los Angeles, the RS was essentially a Z28 Camaro with V-6 power.

Continued from page 91

accents. Suspension upgrades were made, too. The flashy but slow-selling Berlinetta was discontinued midyear after only 4479 of the '86s were made. The 305-cid V-8 that was standard in Z28s and optional down the line got a 10-hp boost to 165.

For 1987, a 350-cid V-8 returned to the Camaro for the first time since 1981. This 5.7-liter TPI powerplant was a $1045 option for the IROC-Z. Available only with the automatic transmission, it made 225 hp at 4400 rpm and could propel a Camaro to 60 mph in 6.3 seconds, with a quarter-mile run in about 14.5 ticks. Also, the five-speed manual became available with the optional 215-horse V-8, but the carbureted 190-hp V-8 was gone.

With the four-cylinder engine cut from Camaros, the 2.8-liter V-6 became the new base engine. A limited number of RS Camaros with Z28 looks but more affordable—and insurable—V-6 power were sold in some markets. The Berlinetta's absence was filled by a series of LT option groups for base models that contained varying levels of luxury and convenience equipment.

The biggest story, though, was the return of convertible Camaros after an 18-year hiatus. Produced with assistance from American Specialty Company, the task of converting a Camaro hatchback coupe into a notch-

Continued on page 99

Opposite: For 1988, the Z28 name went on hiatus again, edged out by the top-line IROC-Z. Pictured here are the high- and low-end of the '88 Camaro lineup: the $18,015 IROC-Z convertible and the $10,995 Sport Coupe. *This page, top:* **The convertible body style wasn't restricted to IROCs—a base Camaro convertible started at $16,255 with standard V-8 power.** *Middle:* **Entry-level Camaros adopted many of the body pieces of the previous year's Z28, but did without the IROC-Z's flashy scooped hood, fog lights, and blacked-out headlamp recesses.** *Bottom:* **IROC-Z buyers could delete the name-logo and stripe decals for a $60 credit. The tuned-port-injection 5.7-liter V-8, now up five hp to 230, was still the top engine option.**

Left: The International Race of Champions still pitted the top drivers from all areas of motorsport in identically prepared IROC-Z race cars. Pictured from left to right are Geoff Brabham, Scott Pruett, Terry Labonte, Al Unser, Jr., Bill Elliott, Rusty Wallace, A.J. Foyt, Rick Mears, Dale Earnhardt, Danny Sullivan, Hurley Haywood, and Richard Petty. Labonte was the 1989 IROC Champion. *Below left:* Camaros were formidable competitors in the IMSA Firestone Firehawk Series, a "showroom stock" class of racing where relatively few modifications were allowed. Savvy performance-minded buyers could order a race-ready 1LE-package Camaro—which included heavy-duty disc brakes, engine oil cooler, and aluminum drive-shaft—direct from the dealer. *Below right:* The $18,945 IROC-Z convertible was the flagship of the 1989 Camaro lineup.

Designed at GM's recently opened Advanced Concepts Center near Los Angeles, the California Camaro concept debuted at the 1989 L.A. Auto Show. The swoopy, futuristic shape presaged the fourth-generation Camaro coming in a few years. Tucked under the radically sloped hood was an all-aluminum 3.1-liter V-6. Scissor-hinge doors with integral tinted-glass roof panels—a wild bit of show-car fancy—made for an almost bubble-top effect.

Continued from page 95

back convertible with manual top added about $4400 to the price tag. Introduced in January, 1007 of the '87s were built across all series. *Motor Trend* predicted the new IROC-Z soft top would be "one of the most desirable cars of [the] decade."

Come 1988, base Camaros took on most of the Z28's appearance with the addition of lower-body extensions, chin and deck spoilers, body-colored external mirror housings, and five-spoke alloy wheels, all standard. The lineup was thinned out as the LT option and the basic Z28 model were dropped. The 170-hp V-8 standard in IROC-Zs and optional in base Camaros swapped its four-pot carburetor for electronic fuel injection. Meanwhile, the IROC's extra-cost 5.0- and 5.7-liter engines got slight

Continued on page 103

Opposite: Steadily falling demand for muscle Camaros amounted to barely more than 24,000 of the 1989 IROC-Zs. *This page, top and above:* The lack of fog lights is a tip-off that this 1990 IROC-Z is equipped with the rare 1LE option group for showroom-stock racing. The package included a special fuel pickup and gas tank baffles so that the engine wouldn't starve in high-speed cornering. *Left:* The RS model took over as the entry-level Camaro for 1989. For 1990, the 135-hp 2.8-liter V-6 was swapped out of RS models in favor of a 140-hp 3.1-liter V-6.

This page, above left: All 1991 Camaros wore redesigned ground-effects panels. RS coupes like this one were by far the most popular, with 79,854 produced. *Above:* RS Camaros could be equipped with the Z28's 16-inch aluminum wheels, which were restyled this year. *Left:* The hottest 1991 Camaros were again Z28s, as Chevrolet stopped participating in the IROC racing series and relinquished its rights to use the name. Z28 coupes wore a tall new spoiler, and were the only Camaros that could be equipped with the topline 245-hp 5.7-liter V-8. *Opposite page:* Z28 convertibles were the rarest mainstream '91 Camaros—just 3203 were built.

Continued from page 99

horsepower boosts. Cars ordered with these engines could also be fitted with new silver- or gold-accented 16-inch aluminum wheels.

Base Camaros gained a new identity in 1989 when the RS nameplate appeared nationwide on entry-level models. Convertibles came with the 170-hp 5.0-liter V-8 as standard equipment. GM's PASS-Key security system (first used in '86 Corvettes) enhanced security. Horsepower ratings of the optional IROC-Z engines depended on both transmission and exhaust system: 195 with automatic, 220 with manual, and 230 with dual exhausts on the 5.0 liter; 230 with single exhaust and 240 with dual exhausts on the automatic-only 5.7 liter available for IROC coupes.

A mandated driver-side airbag arrived for 1990, along with a new standard ohv V-6 engine displacing 3.1 liters and rated at 140 hp. A tilt steering wheel and tinted glass were among additions to the general standard-equipment list; IROC-Zs also gained a limited-slip differential and, on convertibles, 16-inch wheels. The lockup points on the automatic-transmission torque converter were raised in an effort to improve fuel economy, and leather upholstery was newly optional.

With the 1991 Camaros set for a March 1990 debut, production of '90 models was cut off early. Output of the '91s rebounded to 100,000 cars,

but even with the long model year, assemblies trailed the 1989 total by about 10,000. The Z28 was revived and the IROC-Z designation dropped because Chevy did not renew its contract with the IROC series. All '91 Camaros had redesigned ground-effects panels. Z28 coupes got a new, much taller rear spoiler and 16-inch wheels. The 170-hp 5.0-liter V-8 was now reserved for use in RS models. The high-output 5.0 liter—hiked to 230 hp—became the new base engine for Z28s; the optional 5.7 V-8 was perked up to 245 hp.

To celebrate Camaro's 25th anniversary in 1992, Chevy came up with a Heritage Appearance package that included bold hood and deck stripes, a body-color grille, black headlamp recesses, and a decklid badge. (All

'92 Camaros had 25th anniversary emblems on their instrument panels.) RS convertibles again got a standard V-6 after several years of it being a credit option in place of the V-8.

The third-generation Camaro's final year was also one in which General Motors very nearly went broke, threw out its top leaders (chairman Bob Stempel and president Lloyd Reuss, both strong "product guys"), and began a long, painful recovery from previous CEO Roger Smith's dismal decade of misleadership. A lot of product programs were delayed or canceled, and with '92 Camaro output barely topping 70,000 units, it's a miracle that Chevy's ponycar wasn't one of them. In fact, an all-new fourth-generation Camaro was just around the corner.

Opposite: Apart from the Heritage Appearance package, Camaro was a near-rerun for '92, mainly because a new generation was waiting in the wings. It was sorely needed, as suggested by the ponycar's 30.6-percent decline in total sales this model year. *This page, top:* Z28 coupes accounted for 5197 of the 1992 Camaro's 70,008 production run. *Below left and right:* Hood/decklid stripes, body color grille, and black headlamp nacelles were included with the Heritage Appearance package. Here it graces a Z28 coupe and a ragtop RS.

A fresh, fully-redesigned Camaro debuted for
1993, dazzling the public and press alike. But
sales sputtered as the design aged and more-
profitable SUVs took the center stage. This time,
there was no reprieve . . . at least not right away.

FOURTH GENERATION: THE END OF THE ROAD?

Perhaps the most remarkable thing about the Generation IV Camaro is that it ever got built at all. Approval was a long, hard struggle for then-Chevrolet General Manager Jim Perkins and everyone else at Chevy and General Motors who passionately believed in it.

The late 1980s and early '90s were among GM's most turbulent and troubled years. Finance-driven CEO Roger Smith had kicked off an incredibly tough transformation of the corporation from an inefficient collection of car divisions competing mostly among themselves toward a nationally integrated company capable of competing more effectively against an onslaught of imports.

Smith's first major step was his 1984 creation of Buick-Oldsmobile-Cadillac" (BOC) and Chevrolet-Pontiac-Canada (CPC) "super-groups,"

which caused huge confusion and disorganization as product programs were reshuffled and people repositioned. On top of that, pile a steady decline in product quality and the ho-hum, look-alike styling that characterized Smith's cost-driven reign, and it's no surprise that GM's reputation and sales were in terrible shape when Smith turned the tiller over to Robert Stempel in 1989.

By then, design and engineering were well underway on next-generation F-car (Chevy Camaro/Pontiac Firebird) ponycars, whose last major re-do was for 1982. With most GM cars migrating to more fuel-efficient front-wheel drive (fwd), there was a serious effort to design fwd F-cars that would share components and powertrains with fwd coupes and sedans. But that bad idea was soon abandoned.

This page: The 1987 F-14 Tomcat concept vehicle influenced the design direction of the fourth-generation Camaro. The rounded body shapes and "blackout" roof treatment of the 1993 Camaro are already evident here. *Opposite, left:* This sketch by designer Kirk Bennion displays an especially rakish roofline and a wheel design very similar to what eventually was used on the production Z28. *Right:* Sculptors Jerome MacDonald (left) and Mark Richards shape a clay scale model of a Camaro design study.

Major Battle

The year 1989 also saw Perkins, who had left GM for a stint as Toyota's top man in America, return to take over Chevrolet, GM's largest division. "Our product offerings were so stale at that time," he recalls, "our only new cars were the Caprice and the minivan, which didn't give me much to work with. And the [new-for-'88 midsize] Lumina was a disaster."

A strong believer in image-enhancing sports cars, Perkins soon found himself leading desperate battles to save and revamp both Chevy's Corvette sports car and its once-popular Camaro ponycar. "It was a constant hassle trying to get a new Camaro through the system," he says, "because there were so many adversaries against it. I saw the preliminary work that had been done and was convinced that it would excite the press, get a lot of people talking about Chevrolet and GM and rub off on the rest of the product line.

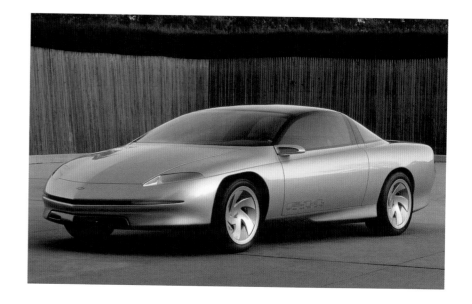

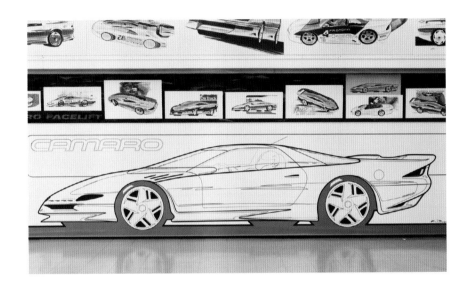

"Dave Hansen was working on it at CPC, but there was a real undercurrent at CPC and at high levels of GM to kill the project. They didn't see the volume opportunity or the investment paying back. Corvette was going through the same thing, so we had a battle on two fronts."

While divisional chief engineer positions were eliminated with the BOC/CPC reorganization, Perkins recruited Hansen from CPC to take over what had been the Chevy chief engineer's responsibilities. "We gave Dave the mission to make sure we made the best possible Camaro," he says, "and we were able to keep it moving forward. And we made I don't know how many revised business cases to sell the project at CPC.

"Because it was a performance car, there was a CAFE (Corporate Average Fuel Economy) issue, the matter of where we would build it, and issues with union concessions that would have to be made. But we kept

grinding on it until we got the volume where we needed it (120,000 for Chevrolet), built a case that made sense, and got the car approved to be built in Canada—given the exchange rate, Canadian labor rates and its composite [body] materials."

Engineering Challenges

Composite body materials? Yes . . . another interesting element of the program. Not counting Corvette, which has always worn composite clothes, the Gen IV F-cars would be GM's fourth go-around with plastic exterior panels. The previous three were the short-lived Pontiac Fiero two-seater, GM's long-nosed "dustbuster" minivans, and the first-generation Saturn small cars. Compared to traditional stamped steel, the advantages of plastic body panels included lower tooling cost, more design

freedom, dent-resistance, and quicker, cheaper styling changes. The disadvantages were slower part production (molding vs. stamping), higher piece cost, and expanding body gaps as adjacent parts contracted in cool temperatures.

All the new Camaro's exterior panels except hoods and rear quarters were plastic—seven different composite materials in all—which brought their share of challenges. "That was a major, major deal," says Ted Robertson, who was F-car platform engineering director at CPC. "Some panels were bonded on, some mechanically attached. And we had many issues with surface quality on the SMC [Sheet Molded Compound] panels, which cost us a lot of time and aggravation."

Robertson took over F-car engineering leadership in 1989, just after the fwd proposal had been killed. CPC Engineering VP Arv Mueller had co-located all his process and product engineers in the old Fisher Body building to enable simultaneous engineering, "which was a great team approach," Robertson relates.

"We formed this super team to do this new F-car and decided to redesign the previous-generation rear-drive vehicle," he says. "We did a new front end and a whole new interior and exterior, and we strengthened the structure, so the rails were new. And it would be the first digital, all-math vehicle in General Motors . . . not just designing it but doing the analysis and everything else in math.

Opposite: Various Gen IV design models are compared to Gen III Camaros in GM's design courtyard. *This page, left:* Getting closer to the final shape; a sculptor makes alterations to a clay model's front fender. Clever use of mirrors enables designers to try out more than one theme on a single clay model. *Below left:* Before the introduction of the California Camaro concept, designers were experimenting with various rear-view mirror designs, as evidenced by the competing treatments on this model. *Below right:* An integrated rear spoiler was another design element inspired by the Tomcat concept vehicle.

This page, above: A proud GM Design staff stands behind the completed 1993 Camaro design model. *Left:* Here, the surfaces of the completed clay model are scanned to acquire the data for production body tooling. *Opposite:* The redesigned Camaro kept to a 101-inch wheelbase, but lower front A-arms returned and four-wheel antilock brakes debuted as standard equipment. Base models came with a new 3.4-liter pushrod V-6 with 160 hp, up 20 from the previous 3.1. Z28s got a version of the LT1 Corvette engine with 275 hp, up 30. It all added up to a more dynamically capable Camaro.

"Our mission was to upgrade everything on the vehicle, make it rakish and stylish, put new engines in it and make sure it meets all new emissions, damageability and MVSS [Motor Vehicle Safety Standard] crash requirements. We had to do coupe and convertible, six-cylinder and eight cylinder, manual and automatic. We upgraded the structure big-time for the convertible and had to make sure the A-pillars, which were raked at a very fast 68 degrees, were strong enough. We used high strength steel and all the latest computer techniques that GM Research had developed."

One challenge was meeting a new side-impact requirement with the longest doors in the industry. Another was achieving "five star" frontal crash-protection. "Because they were sports cars, people had been paying outrageous insurance rates, so I wanted to get those down," Robertson says. "I wanted five-star on these cars, and we got there with new air bags. We also met with insurance companies and the Insurance Institute and showed them how we designed the front end so repair shops could cut off the rails and replace them to keep repair cost down."

The plan to carry over the previous F-cars' rear compartment floor pan to save the cost of new tooling determined the new car's body width. "We had to digitize the existing rear compartment parts and sweeten all the surfaces," he explains. "Everything had to be in math.

"Then, eight or ten months after we designed the car, I went up to Grand Blanc [Michigan], where the rear compartments were made, to look at the dies, and they had been broken and welded up. We would have to do new dies after all, which would cost $5 million."

Engineering Triumphs

Most of Robertson's Gen IV F-car engineering stories have happier endings. One involves the car's high-strength-steel front shock towers. After driving an early engineering vehicle at GM's Mesa, Arizona, Desert Proving Grounds and having it raised on a hoist, he noticed "witness" marks where the front suspension upper control arm rivets were hitting the top of the shock tower. High-speed camera analysis showed that the shock towers were "doming" over potholes and would need to be strengthened. They were quickly redesigned and reinforced.

Another is how it got Torsen differentials: "I was not happy with our rear axles because we always had issues with noise and durability, so I researched around. Then Torsen asked me to come to their plant to see their product. I knew racers used Torsen diffs, which are almost like positraction, and they asked if we would be interested in them. I said no way . . . too costly, too heavy.

"Six months later, I got a call from the Torsen guy. He said, 'You told us we were too expensive and too heavy, so we've redesigned.' And they had done a marvelous job. We got a couple units and put them in test cars. They were lightweight, no gear noise, great durability, and they matched our price. That is how Torsen differentials got into those cars, optional initially and later across the board."

Opposite, above: Camaros came only as coupes for 1993. A base model like the one shown here started at $13,399. *Opposite, below:* The Z28's Corvette-derived LT1 V-8 (left) was even better for '93, thanks to a new, more-precise sequential fuel-injection system and newly computerized ignition timing. The base Camaro's new 3.4-liter V-6 (right) was essentially a bored-out 3.1 with higher compression, and, like the V-8, sequential-port fuel injection. *This page, above:* In addition to the LT1 V-8, the Z28's $16,779 base price included standard 4-wheel disc brakes, 16-inch aluminum wheels, and Z28 badges. *Left:* The new '93 Camaro dashboard earned plaudits for its more logical layout and easy-reach knobs and switches. Safety mavens hailed the newly standard dual front airbags.

Another explains the welcome upgrade to high-gas-pressure monotube shocks. Robertson was driving development vehicles with engineer Norm Fugate on the old oval track at GM's Milford, Michigan, Proving Grounds, and the cars' rear axles were jumping sideways (as always) when cornering over bumps and tar strips.

"The solid rear axle was part of that rear-module carryover," he relates. "We had looked at independent rear suspension but couldn't afford it. We had designed a beautiful new front suspension, and I wanted to fix the rear. Solid axles tend to track better and were better for racing, but otherwise they were the car's Achilles' heel. We had to do something, so I asked Norm what we could do.

"He said, 'Monotube shocks . . . but we don't have budget.' I said, 'That's racing stuff. How much are they?' He said, '35 bucks a corner.'

"I said, 'Put some on the car and let's see what it does.' He did, and we could plant that rear axle. Handling, stability, everything was so much better. We had to put them on the car."

Luckily, GM's Delco Division had just come to an agreement for some monotube shocks with De Carbon of France and was considering buying the company. Robertson told his executive team that he needed to put monotubes on at least the rear of the car and had then-CPC Group Vice President Lloyd Reuss drive a monotube-shock-equipped car on the oval track. Reuss took it over the tar strips and said, "Wow. This is really good, what did you do?"

"Monotube shocks," Robertson said. So GM bought De Carbon, "and we tuned those shocks and put them on the F-cars—standard across the board, front and rear—and that gave us the great ride. That was the start of General Motors putting monotube shocks on vehicles."

Another interesting story involves the Z28's Getrag-sourced six-speed manual transmission. GM designed it, paid for the tooling, and mated it to the Corvette's 5.7-liter aluminum engine. "A great transmission," he says, "still used today."

Then Chrysler called. "They were doing the Viper and didn't have a

Opposite: **The new Camaro was a logical choice for 1993 Indianapolis 500 pace car. The actual pace cars—three were built— were Z28s fitted with a roll bar, strobe lights, safety harness, fire extinguisher, and special upholstery. Chevy offered 645 limited-edition replicas for retail sale. Here, the '93 pace car poses with its '67, '69, and '82 forerunners.** *This page:* **Camaros dominated SCCA Trans Am racing in the early Nineties. Here, Jack Baldwin wheels his Hot Wheels Camaro through a turn in front of the Rain-X Camaro of Scott Sharp. Sharp would go on to win the 1993 Trans Am championship.**

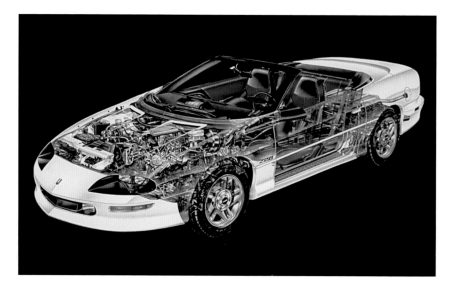

transmission that could handle the V-10 engine, so they asked if they could use ours. Their volume would be low, but they were going to introduce the Viper two or three months before we brought out the new Camaro/Firebird. They said they would give us credit, so I approved them using it."

Dramatic Styling

Meanwhile, the Gen IV Camaro's dramatic exterior look was coming together with influence from two concept cars. "We did a car called Tomcat in the advanced area," says Jerry Palmer, GM's Advanced Design executive director at the time. "Clark Lincoln was the chief designer, Ken Okyama the young designer who did the sketches and got us going. I'm a firm believer that competition improves the breed, so we wanted to get a little competition going between the advanced and production studios. The production studio had its hands full, so we got a head start and did some studies of proportions and a very fast windshield."

Jim Bieck, a chief designer in John Schinella's California GM Advanced Concepts Center, did a much wilder concept. "It was a knock-out," Palmer

Opposite, top: After a year's hiatus, the ragtop Camaro returned for 1994 sharing the basic design of the new fourth-generation coupe. A cutaway illustration by Dave Kimble highlights the construction and layout of the Z28 version. A power soft top with heated glass rear window was standard for both the base and Z28 models. *Bottom:* Interiors were little-changed overall for '94, but manual-shift Z28s inherited the Corvette's Computer Aided Gear Selection feature that "forced" a change from first to fourth gears on light-throttle as a fuel-economy aid. *This page:* A 1995 Z28 convertible started at $23,095. This example wears Sebring Silver Metallic, a new-for-'95 color.

This page: For 1995, Z28s (top) got Corvette's traction control system (called Acceleration Slip Regulation) as a $450 option. Midway through the model year, a 200-hp 3.8-liter V-6 became available as an option to the standard 160-hp 3.4 in base Camaros (above). *Opposite:* For 1996, the 3.4-liter V-6 was dropped and the 3.8 became standard in base Camaros. The Z28's 16-inch aluminum wheels were a $275 option that could give a V-6 Camaro a little extra pizzazz.

says. "Most notable were its high front fenders that led into the mirrors. It had great proportions with a long wheelbase, a very short rear overhang and fantastic scissor doors. But it was a pure concept vehicle, a sketch that became a running car, not a serious production proposal. It violated some things from an engineering standpoint that we couldn't do with a production vehicle."

The Tomcat was completed before John Cafaro's Chevrolet #2 Studio started on the production car and was available for inspiration in fiberglass model form. The California Camaro was a secret project that then-Design Vice President Chuck Jordan threw up against Cafaro's nearly finished production-intent car at the last minute.

"That was a very emotional deal," Cafaro recalls, "because Chuck kept it hidden from us. We were working on our car to go to production and just about ready to release it and freeze the surfaces. Then Chuck said, 'Wait a minute, I'm going to show you the way it really ought to be done.'

"I wasn't in the studio when they had the big Chuck Jordan review. He lambasted everybody there. He said our car sucked, we didn't know what we were doing, and this was the way to go. But that car was an advanced design cartoon with gigantic wheels and no engineering criteria. It was great, but not doable, and that ruffled a lot of feathers. We couldn't really change our car. It was pretty much done. The only thing we did incorporate from the California Camaro were those mirror pods where the mirrors are built into the fenders.

"It could have been more influential if we had known about it ahead of time. It could have been more of a collaboration instead of a hidden agenda. We made a sincere effort to try to bake in some of its innovative features, but it had no impact on the interior . . . or on the exterior, other than that mirror thing."

One major challenge was the extremely "fast" 68-degree windshield. "Chuck liked very aggressive, fluid designs and fast windshields," Cafaro says. "We wanted the proportions to be the best we could do at the time," Palmer adds. "We were after an extremely fast windshield, and it wound up with one of the fastest of any production vehicle, including

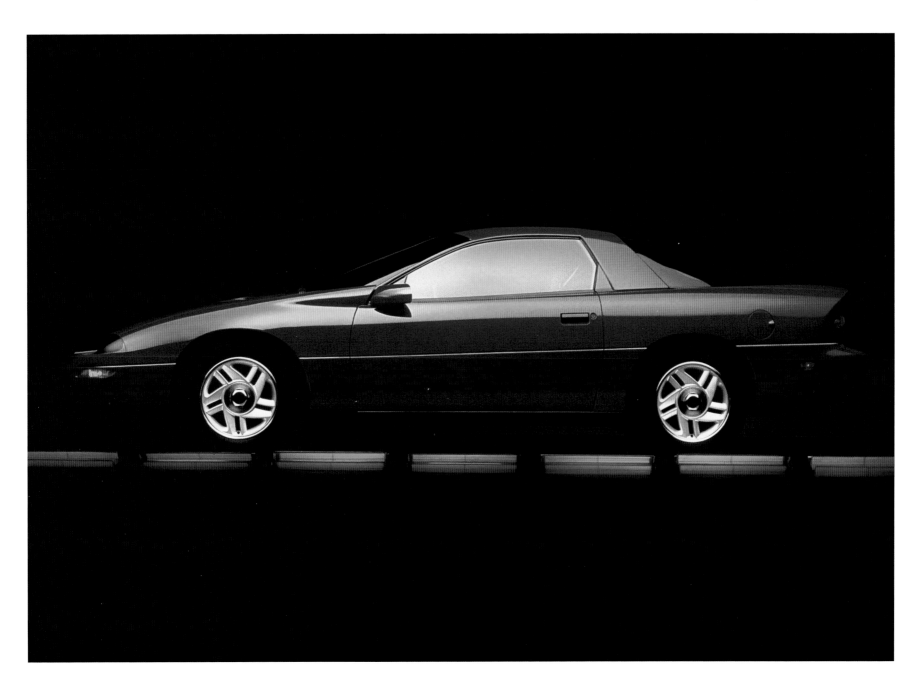

Corvette. That was one thing we fought hard for and did a lot of work on in the advanced area."

Cafaro relates that this car was an exterior-driven design generated from outside to inside that was "zoomier" than previous Camaros but more "claustrophobic" in visibility from the interior. Also, the design did not originally comprehend that very fast windshield. "That drove a whole new front of dash," he says, "which was a manufacturing issue, and a lot of investment to redevelop that area and re-package the wipers. We were in the midst of those 'dustbuster' minivans with that long instrument panel that a lot of people didn't like, so we were very cognizant of how fast is too fast. But it sure looked good from the outside."

The car's low, pointy nose and swoopy roofline brought additional challenges. One was getting the hoodline down and the powertrain packaged beneath it. "They worked very hard on keeping the engine and components low enough to get almost a mid-engine look and still have a big V-8 under the hood," Cafaro says, "and that work ultimately found its way into the fifth generation Corvette." Another was fitting a proper Camaro face—"kind of a sneering quarterback look with black under the eyes," Cafaro calls it—onto the vertically narrow nose. On the other hand, the car's composite front fenders enabled some "very interesting" shapes.

"And the rear styling was pretty innovative," he adds. "The advanced studio was looking at backlights that slipped underneath a floating wing. Ken Okuyama did it on a model called the Stealth, then translated that into the Tomcat concept. That was a challenge to engineer, but Chuck liked it, and we liked it, so we embraced it and built it into the car."

Launch

"We finally got the car approved and launched, and it did what we expected," says then-Chevy General Manager Perkins. While it launched into a market that had seen Camaro sales slip from more than 200,000 in 1984 to about 55,000 in 1991 and 70,000 in 1992, he was optimistic that such a vastly improved new car would lead to much-improved sales, even as its

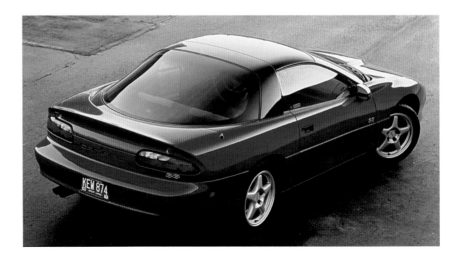

Opposite, top: The Z28's LT1 V-8 was up 10 horsepower to 285 for 1996, thanks in part to more-efficient sequential fuel injection. *Opposite, middle and bottom:* If a 285-hp Z28 wasn't enough, buyers could now choose a new Z28 SS with a 305-hp LT1, unique hood with functional forced-induction hood scoop, upgraded suspension, and 17-inch Corvette ZR-1-style wheels. Though the $3999 SS package was available through Chevrolet dealers, the modifications were actually performed by aftermarket tuning specialist SLP Engineering of Troy, Michigan. *This page:* A tradition continued; Camaro became the first (and at that time only) car to pace five races at Indianapolis when this special coupe did the honors at the 1996 NASCAR Brickyard 400. The nostalgic graphics treatment recalled the 1969 Indianapolis 500 pace car, right down to the houndstooth-pattern seat inserts. Note the unique strobe-light pod at the rear of the roof.

Opposite: **New five-spoke wheels and a revised interior were among the updates to the 1997 Camaro. Sadly, total sales dropped for the calendar year to just under 55,000 units.** *This page:* **Rally Sport Camaros in both coupe and convertible body styles rejoined the Camaro lineup for 1996 and were continued for '97. As before, RSs offered extra flash, but not extra performance; their unique features included front and rear fascias, "ground-effects" side skirts, and a three-piece rear spoiler.**

target customers were moving in increasing numbers into trucks and SUVs.

It debuted in standard and Z28 coupe versions, longer, lower, and wider than its predecessor, while retaining its 101.1-inch wheelbase. A 160-hp 3.4-liter V-6 was standard with 4-speed automatic or 5-speed manual. A 275-hp version of the Corvette's 5.7-liter LT1 V-8, with a choice of 4-speed automatic or the new six-speed manual, powered the Z28.

Suspension was a new short/long arm (SLA) design in front and much-improved multi-link (two trailing arms, track bar, and torque arm) axle in back. New Goodyear Eagle all-season tires on 16-inch wheels and power rack-and-pinion steering (replacing the previous recirculating ball) provided much better responsiveness, feel, and feedback on both models. Brakes were power front disc/rear drum on the standard coupe, 4-wheel discs on the Z28.

That May, a Z28 Camaro paced the Indianapolis 500 for the fourth time. "We did a lot of work with it there and had a tremendous event," Perkins recalls. "People went nuts over the car, and we got a lot of press.

Refreshment Cycle?

"So, it launched well, and for the first couple of years, we did very well with it," he continues. Beyond that, we planned a refreshment cycle that made sense, doing just enough to keep the car fresh. Then we got into the discussion about all the other work to be done, all the other products we were trying to move through the system that had been delayed due to GM's financial struggles, and some that needed freshened and cleaned up, including the new Lumina. So as money and engineering resources got tighter, the Camaro began to suffer."

So changes were mostly evolutionary through the 1997 model year: addition of a convertible model and sequential port fuel injection on the LT1 for '94; optional Acceleration Slip Regulation (ASR) traction control for '95; an optional 3800 fuel-injected V-6 and a new RS appearance package for '96; standard 3800 V-6 and a 30th Anniversary Z28 package (Hugger Orange stripes on Arctic White) reminiscent of the 1969 Indy pace car for '97.

Continued on page 129

This page: Chevy celebrated Camaro's 30th birthday by offering a special 30th Anniversary package that mimicked the look of the 1996 Brickyard 400 pace car. Available on both coupes and convertibles, the package included Arctic White paint set off by eye-popping Hugger Orange stripes on the hood, roof, and tail, plus black badging and white 16×8 five-spoke aluminum wheels. Cloth seat inserts picked up the nostalgic houndstooth pattern that was optional on 1969 Camaros. All '97 Camaros wore a 30th Anniversary headrest logo. *Opposite:* This prototype 30th Anniversary Camaro SS wears a reverse color scheme and chrome wheels.

This page: Camaros were facelifted for 1998 with a more sculpted nose and composite headlights. Z28s got something else new under that reshaped hood: a version of the Corvette's aluminum LS1 V-8. It made 305 hp standard, 320 with the SS package. *Opposite left:* This 1999 ragtop wears the $1755 Sport Appearance Package, which included 16-inch aluminum wheels, ground-effects body add-ons, and an extended rear spoiler. *Right:* The 2000 Camaro 302 Concept recalled the muscle Camaros of yore with a hot-rodded LS1-based V-8 that put out 435 horsepower. A T-56 six-speed transmission, limited-slip 4.10:1 rear end, beefed-up suspension, and 18-inch American Racing Torq-Thrust II wheels were among its other high-performance features.

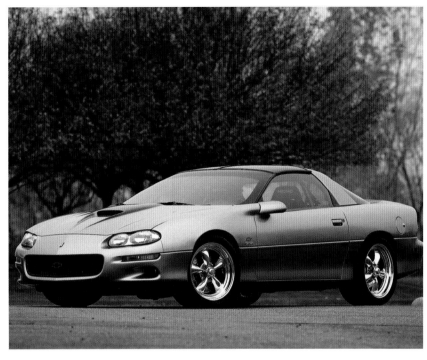

Continued from page 125

For '98, Camaro got a modest facelift with a new front fascia, grille, and hood that gave it almost a Ferrari-look face. "I was involved with John Cafaro on that," Palmer relates, "because I was running Chevrolet, Pontiac and Advanced Design at that time. I felt it needed a little more substantial front end. The original car was so piercing in profile, it wouldn't hurt to chunk it up a bit. So this one was less severe, had larger headlamps and a Ferrari-like grille."

"We were trying to do a throwback to the '70½," Cafaro adds, "with the center aperture and blistered lights. But because we did it on such an aggressive proportion, it ended up looking like a Ferrari. When we did the SS version with the neat NACA hood scoop, it looked even more like a Ferrari. We just tried to freshen it up, inject a little newness into it and bring back some strong Camaro cues. We were also trying to improve quality at that time."

Perkins says even that minor change was a major struggle to get approved. "We just couldn't freshen it up, didn't have money or resources. That one finally happened after I left [in 1996]," he recalls. "We had it on the board since '95. We got a little of the prominent-nose Gen II look that we wanted, but not nearly as much as we had hoped for. That would have required a complete new front end, hood, fenders and grille. And there were some things we wanted to do to the rear. We had some stupid low budget allotted to it, and where could we get engineering resources? It was a compromise to be able to do anything. It did alright and held up for a while, but never could sustain the volume it needed."

That facelifted '98 Camaro also got a Sport Appearance Package replac-

This page: Speeders beware! The B4C Special Service Package outfitted a Camaro for "pursuit capable" police work with heavy-duty components and Z28-spec hardware. Just 288 were built for 2001, including nine with the six-speed manual transmission. *Opposite:* V-8 Camaros added five horses for '01, lifting the Z28 to 310 and the SS (shown) to 325. But Chevy's ponycar continued losing sales ground to the rival Ford Mustang, which only intensified rumors of Camaro's imminent demise.

ing the former RS, a 305-hp version of the new-for-'97 Corvette's LS1 V-8 for the Z28 and an SS Performance/Appearance Package that boosted it to 320 galloping horses. Its four-wheel disc brakes, ABS, and ASR systems were also new and/or improved. For 2001, this marvelous engine was conservatively rated at 310 hp in the standard Z28 and 325 in the Z28 SS—both numbers intentionally held lower than Corvette's as a result of a lower-lift *truck* camshaft.

Cafaro (a racer himself) adds that his studio "did a lot of neat stuff" with racing the Gen IV Camaro. "Randy Wittine did the race-car body in the basement—unbeknownst to Wayne Cherry [who became GM's fifth Design VP when Jordan retired]—that I think was one of the best Trans Am racers in terms of sticking to the production silhouette. We got into SCCA [Sports Car Club of America] Trans Am big time with some really exciting graphics. It was a very vibrant period when design was interacting with motorsports and a lot of fun. The cars looked great and went well,

and there were great battles with Ford. That was a renaissance of Trans Am and IMSA [International Motor Sports Association] production-based road racing."

The End . . . or Was It?

But U.S. sporty coupe sales continued to slip as truck and SUV sales mushroomed. Despite Corvette-like performance and handling, Camaro was being badly outsold by arch-rival Mustang—partly because it had grown a bit too big, expensive, and aggressive for nonperformance buyers, but mostly because it was getting long in the tooth. "Every time we went through a planning meeting or President's Council meeting, it became an assault on the F-car. So the volumes continued to drop, and the longer that went on, the more of the market Mustang got and the less we got," said Perkins.

With fewer than 50,000 Camaros delivered each year from 1998

This page and opposite: The end of an era; the 2002 farewell-edition 35th Anniversary Camaros came as SS convertibles or T-top coupes in red only. Included in the $2500 package were silver checkered-flag pattern stripes, special fender badges, embroidered headrest logos, and ten-spoke SS wheels with machine-faced surfaces and black accents.

to 2000, and just over 34,000 sold in 2001, it became clear to nearly everyone at GM that Camaro (and sister-ship Firebird) would have to be mercifully, and very reluctantly, put to rest. According to then-GM Vice President Vehicle Brand Marketing John Middlebrook (a car guy and Camaro enthusiast who once ran Chevrolet Division), the combination of significantly reduced demand in the sporty coupe segment—down 53 percent from 1990 to 2000—and substantial excess manufacturing capacity made this decision "unavoidable." In other words, in an increasingly cutthroat competitive market, GM—on a fairly positive roll at the time but still struggling to maintain market share and profitability—needed fewer plants and few (or no) unprofitable products.

"The Chevrolet Camaro and Pontiac Firebird have truly become an integral part of American culture over the years," he said in the cancella-

tion announcement. "We appreciate the strong emotions that our customers have for these cars, and we're pleased to celebrate them with a 35th Anniversary Edition Camaro and a Collector Edition Firebird Trans Am."

Could GM have saved its aging ponycars by redesigning them again, and sooner? Perhaps. But new-product design, engineering, and development is incredibly expensive. And with the ponycar segment continuing to shrink, that would have diverted critically important investment dollars from higher-volume products the company desperately needed to survive.

Would GM revive the Camaro one day? No one knew. But the press release announcing the difficult decision to cancel these once-beloved cars after 35 exciting years began with the headline: "Camaro/Firebird on Hiatus After 2002 Model Year." It was no accident that the word "hiatus" implied a potential return.

After an eight-year hiatus, GM looked to the past for inspiration in crafting an all-new fifth-generation Camaro. Here, The Auto Editors of Consumer Guide® present the fascinating story of an American icon's rebirth.

FIFTH GENERATION: AN ICON REBORN

Well, here we go again. Just as Chevrolet created the 1967 Camaro to take on Ford's hot-selling Mustang, so the all-new 2010 Camaro coupes and 2011 convertibles go after the popular Mustang that galloped in for '05. The Dodge Challenger is back too, treating Detroit loyalists to their first three-way ponycar race since 2002, when the Camaro and sibling Pontiac Firebird were dropped after years of failing to outsell Mustang.

But the past is not entirely prologue here. Where the original ponycars were products of a late-1960s boom economy, the 21st-century trio is born to an America beset by falling home values, declining consumer confidence and purchasing power, rising prices for most everything, intense foreign competition, and fast-changing public attitudes about the environment and the automobile's place in it. All this has made big trouble for the Big Three, which aren't so big anymore. Indeed, since the new century began, Chrysler, Ford, and General Motors had been forced to take painful downsizing measures to cope with mounting losses in sales and earnings. Yet for all the plant closings, layoffs, asset sales, and other cost-cutting moves, each company faces an uncertain future. For now, however, let's forget such doom-and-gloom and focus on the good old-fashioned fun of a brand-new Camaro.

Rebirth

The story begins in early 2005, when top GM executives met to plan their concept vehicles for the January 2006 North American International Auto Show (NAIAS) in Detroit. Among those attending were Ed Welburn, vice-president of global design, and celebrated GM vice-chairman "Maximum Bob" Lutz, head of global product development. Also in the room was Al Oppenheiser, who then headed GM's concept-vehicle development group and would later be named chief engineer for North American rear-wheel-

This page, above: GM designers had 35 years of wonderful heritage from which to choose when concocting the resurrected Camaro—as this "inspiration board" illustrates. As it turned out, almost all of the inspiration came from the classic '69 model. *Above right and opposite:* A handful of early computer-generated design renderings display various takes on the '69 Camaro's iconic styling cues. Exaggerated, almost toy-like proportions with oversized wheels and wildly "chopped" tops are present in all of these free-form exploratory sketches.

drive vehicles, including the 2010 Camaro.

"It takes approximately 40 weeks to do a concept," Oppenheiser told us. "We were well within the 40 weeks and we still hadn't decided what we were going to do. It came down to what brands needed something to show, plus resources, budget, and what production vehicles we were introducing. Remember, we introduced the Corvette Z06 at that show. In the last ten minutes of the meeting, Ed Welburn raised his hand and said, 'If I can do only one stellar concept, I want to do a Camaro.'" That was, perhaps, no surprise, as Welburn was the proud owner of a '69 Camaro SS hardtop.

A more-urgent motivation was the redesigned 2005 Mustang, then speeding toward nearly 161,000 U.S. calendar-year sales, a near 24-percent jump on the model's '04 tally. Sport-utility vehicles might have been the market heavyweights, but if Ford had found a way to reignite ponycar fever—and profits—GM didn't want to be left out. Besides, corporate pride demanded a response, just as in the '60s. Hence the decision to bring the Camaro out of limbo, if only as a test-the-waters concept.

Design Diligence

Initial styling work produced what Oppenheiser termed a "more retro-looking" coupe that evidently failed to excite Welburn or Lutz. Seeking

other ideas, Welburn called in designer Tom Peters, who had recently headed the styling effort for the 2004 Cadillac XLR and 2005 Corvette C6. Peters, another longtime Camaro fan, was "very excited, pleased, and maybe even a little scared" at the assignment. Design a new Camaro? That would be "quite a task," he recalled. But Peters had already assembled a mostly young "diverse team that didn't have this direct understanding of Camaros in the past, so consequently I got some very fresh perspectives." A key player was Sangyup Lee, who'd worked with Peters on the C6 and would later oversee new-Camaro production styling.

Working on a tight six-month deadline, Peters repeated the approach he'd used for the C6. That Corvette took inspiration from the classic '63 Sting Ray split-window coupe. Here, the chosen starting point was the 1969 Camaro coupe. "It just seemed the most pure statement," Peters explained. "The first ones [1967-68 Camaros] were very straightforward, but the '69 was more sophisticated and uniquely American. Nobody told me that's what I should do. I just felt that was the way to approach it. So, as we did with the C6, there's iconic design cues on the '69 that we analyzed, distilled down and reinterpreted in a fresh way." The upshot was that the '69 was just a third-season restyle of the original F-body Camaro, but the makeover—created under famed GM Design veteran Henry Haga—was obviously memorable.

SANGYUP LEE

Interior designers under Jeff Perkins were also looking at the '69. Coincidence? Not really. According to John Zelenak, who supervised production interior work: "We may be sitting in another room, but the walls slide up and there's the exterior guys. So we're always conversing. But the interior always had this very clean, wide cross-car feel. Very simple shapes, very simple forms, easy-to-reach controls [for] performance driving. Now it just so happens that's exactly how you feel in a '69 Camaro. You're sitting low, with a very sinister feel from the high beltline. But nobody told us to mimic the '69. We wanted to do a fresh spin, just like the exterior guys were. And we knew we were going to get what we wanted with the way the exterior was shaping up."

Because time was so limited, the Camaro Concept was built on a modified version of GM's premium rear-drive Sigma platform, familiar from the Cadillac CTS sedan and other models. Though a concept Dodge Challenger vied for attention at NAIAS 2006, the Camaro generated so much enthusiasm that GM committed to a production model barely two months later, around March. The car was publicly announced that August. Meantime, to keep interest stoked, a companion convertible concept was built for the following year's Detroit show. Later in 2007, interest went sky-high and global when the Camaro played a starring role in the summer-blockbuster action film *Transformers*.

SANGYUP LEE

The Road to the Showroom

Transforming the concept design for production would prove a major challenge for all concerned, both technically and logistically. That's because cost factors dictated the production car use the Zeta platform developed by GM's Holden branch in Australia and not the U.S.-devised Sigma architecture. This choice reflected GM's rapid shift to a more cost-effective global product-planning regime in which various regional units took sole responsibility for specific vehicle types and families. Thus, for example, Opel in Europe was assigned to develop GM's compact and midsize cars, while North America handled large trucks. Holden was the designated center for rear-wheel-drive cars, including sporty performance machines like Camaro.

The 14-to-16-hour time difference between GM's Warren, Michigan, Tech Center and Holden's home in Melbourne meant difficult "split-shift" workdays and long plane rides for team members based in each of those far-flung locales. Chassis testing was done mainly in Australia, but there

were extensive ride-and-handling shakedowns on Germany's demanding Nürburgring circuit, a development crucible that also benefited the CTS and C6. What's more, the team solicited the expert opinions of top racing drivers such as NASCAR ace Dale Earnhardt, Jr.; World Touring Car Championship pilot Rob Huff; and Mark Skaife, five-time season champion in Australia's V8 Supercar Series. Also taking the wheel were noted corporate hotshoes such as John Heinricy, head of GM's Performance Group, and Holden managing director Mark Reuss, the son of former GM CEO Lloyd Reuss.

Though many people had to work unusually hard on the new Camaro, their efforts would pay off handsomely. For one thing, the Australia-based team, led by chief engineer Doug Houlihan and vehicle line executive Gene Stefanyshyn, shared Detroit's understanding of what a new Camaro must be and had the talent to make it so. Moreover, as Houlihan told *Automobile* magazine, "The worldwide connection that we now have [with-

This page, above left: An early clay-model proposal for the Camaro Concept exhibited a more literal take on the retro design theme. *Above right:* GM product development honcho Bob Lutz sizes up an early clay mock-up proposal in the GM Design courtyard. Lutz and GM vice-president of global design Ed Welburn later decreed a shift in direction to a less overtly nostalgic motif. *Left:* As always, scale models played an important role in exploring design themes. Adhesive film is used to quickly cover the bare clay and approximate the light reflections of a high-gloss paint job. *Opposite, top left and right:* Both computer numerically controlled (CNC) tools and good old-fashioned hand sculpting were used in the creation of the Camaro Concept clay model. *Bottom right:* Designers Tom Peters (left) and Sangyup Lee examine the in-progress Camaro Concept.

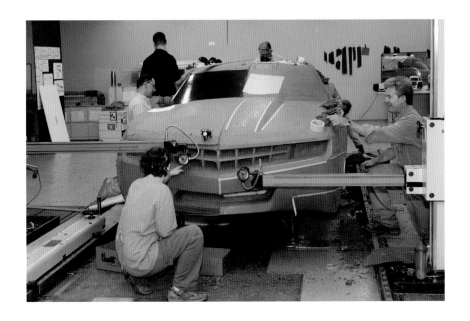

in GM] keeps us from making the same mistakes twice . . . . The key is that we're talking to Detroit—and they're talking to everyone else around the world—on a regular basis."

Perfecting the Platform

No less important was the Zeta platform itself. Officially termed the Global Rear-Wheel-Drive Architecture, it first appeared with two new sports sedans, the 2007 Holden Commodore VE and 2008 Pontiac G8. Despite chassis tuning tailored for two distinct markets, each delivered levels of handling, ride comfort, refinement, and go-power that prompted favorable comparisons with the vaunted BMW 5-Series selling for twice as much. As a foundation for the new Camaro, Zeta was excellent.

Still, all involved were adamant that the production car maintain the concept's stunning looks, and that led to a number of platform changes—enough to merit a "Zeta II" designation. First, the structure had to be resized for the Camaro, which ended up 5.7 inches shorter than the G8 sedan (at 190.4 inch-

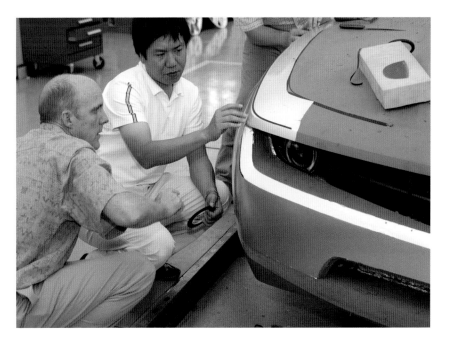

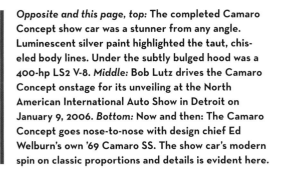

Opposite and this page, top: The completed Camaro Concept show car was a stunner from any angle. Luminescent silver paint highlighted the taut, chiseled body lines. Under the subtly bulged hood was a 400-hp LS2 V-8. *Middle:* Bob Lutz drives the Camaro Concept onstage for its unveiling at the North American International Auto Show in Detroit on January 9, 2006. *Bottom:* Now and then: The Camaro Concept goes nose-to-nose with design chief Ed Welburn's own '69 Camaro SS. The show car's modern spin on classic proportions and details is evident here.

es) on a 2.5-inch trimmer wheelbase (112.3). In addition, Camaro's long-hood/short-deck styling required a three-inch extension of the platform's dash-to-axle dimension, the line running from the foot pedals to the front axle.

In addition, Oppenheiser notes that engineers took the opportunity to stiffen the front and rear subframe mounts to further sharpen handling. And he was very proud of the work with manufacturing colleagues that produced a one-piece "side ring," a unitized bodyside running from the A-pillars back through the rear quarters. Because of its size and complexity, this structure required devising intricate and costly new stamping techniques, but Oppenheiser says the effort preserved the concept design's muscular "shoulders" without the unsightly "ditch molding" at the base of the C-pillar that would have otherwise been required. This construction also contributed to claimed class-leading structural rigidity of 26 hertz in bending and 33 hz in torsion. This, too, would benefit handling, not to mention side-impact strength in government crash tests.

The other big platform change involved the independent rear suspension. IRS is a handling plus almost by definition, but Oppenheiser said the original Zeta setup had to be reengineered to approximate the cost of a solid axle. That was because the Camaro was planned to sell for only a bit

This page, top: GM President North America Troy Clarke introduces the Camaro Convertible Concept at the 2007 Detroit Auto Show. Bottom: California governor Arnold Schwarzenegger (left) gets an up-close look at the 2007 L.A. Auto Show. Opposite: Designers sprinkled in a few more retro styling touches, including a two-tone interior, traditional hood-and-deck stripes, and red-rimmed wheels that hint at '60s redline tires.

more than comparable Mustangs, where solid axles still ruled. The IRS did have higher unsprung mass, he admitted, "but it was worth it to get the levels of ride and handling and the lower noise and vibration we wanted." It also matched a bragging-rights feature of the resurrected Challenger.

The Unveiling

Despite a gestation period of just 26 months—one of the fastest new-model programs in GM's 100-year history—the new Camaro didn't formally meet the press until summer of 2008. That puzzled some who'd seen the Camaro and Challenger concepts debut side-by-side, as Challenger sales began that spring, though only with a limited-run top-line 2008-model SRT8 coupe. Camaro would kick off with 2010-model coupes scheduled to begin full production on February 16, 2009. Convertibles were set to arrive as 2011 models.

A bit tardy it may have been, but the reborn Camaro was more than worth the wait. For starters, it looked sensational, identical to the concept coupe save small reductions in overall width and front overhang, plus an equally imperceptible 0.8-inch-higher roofline. Crash standards precluded a '69-style pillarless hardtop design, so the coupe had fixed B-posts. So did the new Challenger. But where the Dodge seemed deliberately "retro" in appearance, the Camaro followed the contemporary Mustang in instantly evoking thoughts of a famous forebear without copying a single line, form, or dimension. If anything, the Chevy had more visual impact because it referenced only the '69 Camaro, rather than mixing cherry-picked cues from several models like the Ford.

And there were plenty of fresh touches, such as the dropped-center roof section on coupes without optional sunroof. Though you had to be

This page: GM rarely missed an opportunity to keep the public's appetite whetted for the forthcoming production Camaro. Here, Chairman and CEO Rick Wagoner takes the Camaro Convertible Concept out for a joy-ride at the 2007 Woodward Avenue Dream Cruise in Royal Oak, Michigan. *Opposite, top:* The reborn Camaro had a starring role as "Bumblebee" in 2007's *Transformers.* Because the actual Camaro was at least two years from production, the movie cars were actually rebodied 2006 Pontiac GTOs. *Bottom left:* Bumblebee also took the stage with fashion models at the 2008 edition of the GM Style event—an annual General Motors fashion and music gala that kicks off the North American International Auto Show. *Bottom right:* Camaro interior designer Micah Jones stands with a "life-size" image of the transformed Bumblebee in the GM Design Center.

looking down on the car to appreciate it, the "debossed" area neatly picked up the line of the prominent bonnet bulge recalling Camaro's reverse-facing "cowl-induction" hood of yore. A quartet of half-moon tail-lamps was another departure, but the triple rear-fender hashmarks, full-width vee'd grille and low ground-hugging stance were pure '69.

The interior continued the fresh-but-familiar theme. Its only real visual throwbacks were squarish main instrument nacelles and a console-mount gauge pack. The latter, recalling a similar option for the '69 Camaro, comprised analog dials for oil pressure, oil temperature, battery charge, and transmission-fluid temperature. Everything else inside was new-century modern. There was even a fold-down back seat. A literal highlight was the optional ambient-lighting package with translucent acrylic panels on the dashboard and doors. LEDs in a concealed "light pipe" washed these

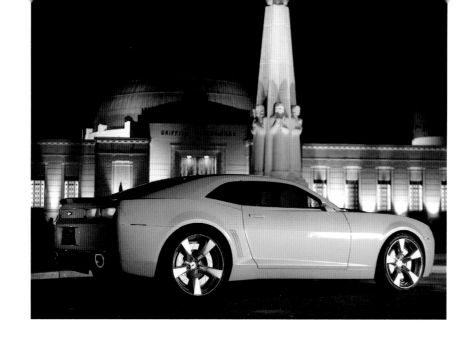

This page, above: Bob Lutz, Rick Wagoner, and GM President and COO Fritz Henderson stand next to an in-progress clay model of the production Camaro. Wagoner announced that Chevrolet would produce the car on August 10, 2006. *Above right:* Sangyup Lee and Tom Peters discuss a scale model of the production Camaro. Judging from the hood scoop and aggressive front fascia, this is likely an SS-model proposal. *Right:* Two 2010 Camaro design prototypes display competing front-fascia treatments. Note the "two-face" mock-up on the car at right. *Opposite:* Computer renderings of the 2010 Camaro interior display the optional ambient lighting package and console-mounted gauge cluster.

panels in a restful ice-blue color to impart a real high-tech look after dark. Equally impressive was the extensive use of low-gloss soft-touch interior plastics applied by a newly developed spray process. It made a vast difference in perceived quality over that of even 2002 Camaros.

Model Breakdown

Camaro returned with three basic coupe models: V-6 LS, a step-up LT version, and V-8 SS. All matched the competition for general size (see sidebar, page 158), but only the Chevys claimed standard antiskid/traction control—GM's well-regarded Stabilitrak, of course. The Camaro system offered three modes including full off, which delighted leadfoots. V-8s added a "competitive/sport" setting that raised the stability control's

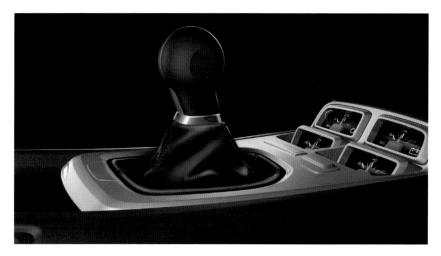

intervention speed to permit a little tail-sliding for those so inclined (and hopefully skilled). A limited-slip differential was standard for all models except V-6/automatics. Manual-shift V-8s came with a "launch-control" function that allowed full-throttle takeoffs with minimum wheelspin for quickest acceleration.

Standard four-wheel antilock disc brakes were expected of modern sports cars, and all Camaros had them. The SS got slightly larger rotors clamped by four-piston Brembo-brand calipers. The ABS tied into another electronic driving aid called Engine Drag Control. This monitored any difference between front and rear wheel speeds, as can happen when lifting the throttle on a low-friction surface. In the event, EDC would send more torque to the rear wheel with better grip to help restore or maintain stability.

Suspension geometry was much like the Pontiac G8 sedan's, with front struts, a rear multilink arrangement, all-around coil springs, and a hollow anti-roll bar at each end (the last slightly larger for SS). V-6 models received FE2 suspension tuning, while V-8s got unique FE3 calibrations. All models boasted variable-rate rack-and-pinion steering geared for a quick 2.5 turns lock-to-lock. The rack was mounted ahead of the front axle line to enhance precision and feedback.

Standard footwear naturally varied with model, but all factory tires had the same rolling circumference to preserve the desired "big wheel" look regardless of rim size or trim level. V-8s came with staggered-width 20-inch alloy wheels wearing Z-rated Pirelli summer radials sized at 245/45 fore, 275/40 aft. V-6s had standard 18-inch steel rims and offered optional alloys in the same 7.5-inch width, plus 8-inch-wide 19- and 20-inch alloys. The larger rims wore W-rated all-season Pirelli shoes, P245/50R19s or P245/45R20s. The base tires were P245/55R18 all-season Goodrich. Buyers could also get 20-inch alloys by ordering the RS appearance package, another nod to Camaro's past. This delivered specific midnight-silver 20s, plus high-intensity headlamps, unique taillamps, a discreet decklid spoiler, and the requisite RS badges.

Opposite: Camaros are about as all-American as a car can get, but the 2010 model benefited from a decidedly international upbringing. Since the Camaro's Zeta platform was developed by GM's Australian subsidiary Holden, chassis development and testing took place "Down Under." Development mules were a favorite target of spyphoto "paparazzi"; GM eventually stopped camouflaging them and issued an "official" preproduction spy photo. *This page:* Extensive ride-and-handling shakedown runs were conducted at Germany's challenging Nürburgring road course.

Probable Performance

On paper, the new Camaros had big competitive advantages in standard horsepower (see sidebar, page 158). V-6 models carried GM's much-praised 3.6-liter all-aluminum twincam engine with variable-valve timing, both intake and exhaust, plus direct fuel injection as another class exclusive. With 300 estimated horsepower, it had the same muscle as Mustang's base V-8 and trumped the Challenger's V-6 by a hefty 50 hp. SS models carried one of two 6.2-liter V-8s, the latest in the long line of legendary Chevy small-blocks. Cars with the Tremec 6060 six-speed manual transmission ran the LS3 motor from the contemporary base Corvette, tuned for a stout 422 estimated hp. SS models with six-speed automatic used an L99 V-8 with 400 estimated horses and GM's gas-saving Active

Fuel Management cylinder-deactivation system. Challenger's 5.7 Hemi didn't match those numbers, and its 6.1-liter version was little more potent.

Equally notable, all Camaro engines teamed with six-speed transmissions while rivals settled for four- or five-speed automatics, and non-Shelby Mustangs made do with five-speed manuals. In addition, the SS automatic—GM's Hydra-Matic 6L80, basically a beefed-up version of the 6L50 unit available for V6s—featured steering-wheel "TAPshift" paddles for best-of-both-worlds flexibility.

Comparisons of preliminary performance figures made the 2010 Camaros look like the winners of the modern ponycar race. Chevy estimated V-6s would do 0-60 mph in 6.1 seconds with automatic or manual transmission. That compares with 6.9 seconds for a manual V-6 Mustang

Opposite: **Camaro LS models came standard with a direct-injection 3.6-liter V-6 with variable valve timing and an estimated 300 hp (left). SS models with a six-speed manual packed a 422-hp 6.2-liter LS3 V-8. Automatic SSs got a 400-hp L99 variant (shown).** *This page:* **Camaro's sophisticated new structure included a multilink independent rear suspension with coil-over shock absorbers and a dual ball-strut front suspension with direct-acting stabilizer bar.**

in *Consumer Guide®* tests and 8.1 seconds for a four-speed-automatic Challenger SE sampled by *Edmunds.com.* The Camaro SS was projected to clock a sizzling 4.7 seconds with automatic and 4.9 with manual. That compared with 4.8 for an automatic SRT8 Challenger and 5-flat for a manual 315-hp Mustang Bullitt coupe in a July 2008 *Car and Driver* matchup. Respective quarter-mile times for those cars were 13.3 and 13.6 seconds. Chevy projected the manual/automatic SS to run 13.4/13.3 seconds. Incidentally, all 2010 Camaros pulled a 3.27:1 rear-axle ratio save the manual SS, which had 3.45:1 gearing.

Though enthusiasts always argue acceleration numbers, Camaro returned in the wake of record gas prices, so fuel economy had come to have bragging rights too. Chevrolet initially predicted EPA highway mileage of 27 mpg for V-6 Camaros, highly creditable considering their performance.

But can any of today's ponycars survive long-term in a world concerned about climate change and future energy shortages? And will the all-important post-Baby Boom generations embrace a type of car their parents and

Continued on page 157

This page, left: Ed Welburn (left) and Chevrolet Vice President Ed Peper pose with the production 2010 Camaro on July 21, 2008, the day of its unveiling. Below and opposite: The Rally Sport appearance package included high-intensity headlamps with integrated "halo rings," a subtle decklid spoiler, specific taillights, badges, and 20-inch wheels. The RS package was available on both LTs (seen here in Victory Red and Rally Yellow) and SSs. All 2010 Camaros had dual exhausts, but V-6 versions had smaller exhaust tips than their V-8-powered siblings.

Opposite and this page: When finished in the available Silver Ice Metallic paint color, the 2010 Camaro really captured the look of the original 2006 concept car. SS upgrades included larger four-wheel disc brakes with Brembo-brand four-piston calipers, sport suspension tuning, and a unique front fascia with an integral air scoop and a more-pronounced spoiler. For more-extroverted types, a raft of spoilers, stripes, ground-effects kits, and other dealer-installed dress-up parts were set to go on sale after the '10 Camaros started hitting the streets.

Continued from page 153

grandparents grew up with? While nobody could answer the first question at this writing, Camaro product manager Cheryl Pilcher was optimistic about bridging the generational divide. "Our [older] enthusiast buyers are probably more inclined to V-8 models," she told us at the production Camaro's summer 2008 press unveiling. "But I see a great opportunity for the V-6 models to reach younger buyers who don't know the Camaro legacy, but see a great-looking car with great fuel economy and all the standard safety features they expect. So I see us appealing to men and women in their 20s, 30s, 40s. To them the Camaro may seem like a whole new kind of Chevrolet—which is really what it is. It's so dramatic, you can't help but look at it."

The Bottom Line

Chevrolet announced base prices of $22,995 for a base LS and $30,995 for an SS model. Those numbers were slightly above comparable Challenger and Mustang stickers, but the Camaros were arguably better equipped. They also promised superior build quality, as production was assigned to GM's facility in Oshawa, Ontario, Canada, among the top-rated North American auto plants in independent audits of productivity and vehicle quality.

There were options, of course, but fewer than in the good old days, a reflection of prevailing buyer preferences. Key factory items included a remote engine-start system, operable from the keyfob from more than 300 feet away; ultrasonic rear-park-assist obstacle detection; three-level heated front seats; leather upholstery; and, for the SS, a premium

2010 CHEVROLET CAMARO VERSUS 1969 CAMARO AND MODERN COMPETITORS

	1969 Chevrolet Camaro	2010 Chevrolet Camaro	2009 Dodge Challenger	2009 Ford Mustang
Wheelbase (in.)	108.0	112.3	116.0	107.1
Overall length (in.)	186.0	190.4	197.7	187.6
Overall width (in.)	74.0	75.5	75.7	73.9
Overall height (in.)	51.6	54.2	57.1	55.4
Curb weight, six (lbs)	3,120	3,737	3,720	3,352
Curb weight, V-8 (lbs)	—	—	4,041	3,345
Base six, cid/induction	230/1 bbl.[1]	217/DFI	215/PFI	245/PFI
Compression ratio	8.5:1	11.3:1	10.0:1	9.7:1
Horsepower @ rpm	140 @ 4400[2]	300 @ 6400	250 @ 6400	210 @ 5300
Torque (lb-ft) @ rpm	220 @ 1600	273 @ 5200	250 @ 3800	240 @ 3500
Std. transmission	3-sp M	6-sp M	4-sp A	5-sp M
Opt. transmission	4-sp M, 3-sp A	6-sp A	na	5-sp A
Base V-8, cid/induction	307/2 bbl.	376/PFI	345/PFI	281/PFI
Compression ratio	9.0:1	10.7:1	10.5:1	9.8:1
Horsepower @ rpm	200 @ 4600	422 @ 5000[3]	372 @ 5200[4]	300 @ 5750
Torque (lb-ft) @ rpm	—	408 @ 4500[5]	401 @ 4400[6]	320 @ 4500
Std. transmission	3-sp M	6-sp M	5-sp A	5-sp M
Opt. transmission	4-sp M, 3-sp A	6-sp A	6-sp M	5-sp A
Suspension, front	double A-arm, coil springs	coil-over struts, two lower lateral links, stabilizer	coil-over struts, two lower lateral links, stabilizer	struts, lower control arm, stabilizer
Suspension, rear	live axle, semi-elliptic leaf springs	four-link ind., coil springs, stabilizer	five-link ind., coil springs, stabilizer	three-link solid axle, coil springs, Panhard rod, stabilizer
Steering	recirculating-ball	rack-and-pinion	rack-and-pinion	rack-and-pinion
Std. brakes, front/rear	drum/drum	disc/disc[7]	disc/disc[8]	disc/disc[8]

1. Inline. All others vee-type. 2. SAE gross figures for '69, others SAE net. 3. With manual transmission. With automatic transmission, hp is 400. 4. With automatic transmission. With manual transmission, hp is 376 @ 5150 rpm. 5. With manual transmission. With automatic transmission, torque is 395 lb-ft @ 4500 rpm. 6. With automatic transmission. With manual transmission, torque is 410 lb-ft @ 4300 rpm. 7. With ABS. 8. With ABS on V-8 models. ABS optional with V-6. DFI=direct fuel injection. PFI=port fuel injection. M=manual. A=automatic.

nine-speaker Boston Acoustics audio system. GM's Service and Parts Operation (SPO) developed many other tempting "personal" extras available through dealers: assorted bright exterior moldings, a high-rise spoiler, a racy "ground effects" styling package, 21-inch wheels, rally and "hood and hockey" stripes, engine covers in a choice of five colors, and functional performance enhancers including a tuned air intake, catback exhaust, shorty headers and—shades of '69—a Hurst-brand short-throw shifter.

That's the 2010 Camaro story so far, but we can't leave without a word about the 2011-model convertibles. Again, we don't have full details yet, but LT and SS versions should be listed with the same powertrains and features as equivalent coupes. Just as nice, GM photos of prototypes testing in Australia confirm a fabric roof that power-folds into a compact space and looks Germanically classy when raised. Top-down, of course, the open-air Camaros will look every bit as glamorous as the showstopping Hugger Orange 2007 concept convertible.

With such happy news on the horizon, let's hope today's economic clouds give way to sunny skies for General Motors and all Detroit—and the sooner, the better. Losing Camaro once was bad enough. Losing it again would be a crime.

Top left: The 2010 Camaro's interior was a knockout blend of the fresh and the familiar. Available comfort and convenience features included heated seats, satellite radio, USB port for digital music players, steering-wheel-mounted audio controls, and Bluetooth wireless cell phone link. *Top right and above:* Classy-looking ragtops were scheduled to join the Camaro lineup for 2011. Production models will differ slightly from the preproduction prototypes shown here.